Learning to Pass

# New CLAiT 2006
### Creating an e-presentation

Unit 5

**Ruksana Patel**

**www.heinemann.co.uk**
✓ Free online support
✓ Useful weblinks
✓ 24 hour online ordering

**01865 888058**

**Heinemann**
*Inspiring generations*

Heinemann Educational Publishers
Halley Court, Jordan Hill, Oxford OX2 8EJ
Part of Harcourt Education

Heinemann is the registered trademark of
Harcourt Education Limited

Text © Ruksana Patel, 2005

First published 2005

10 09 08 07 06 05
10 9 8 7 6 5 4 3 2 1

British Library Cataloguing in Publication Data is available
from the British Library on request.

10-digit ISBN: 0 435 082 66 3
13-digit ISBN: 978 0 435 082 66 6

**Copyright notice**
All rights reserved. No part of this publication may be reproduced in any form or by any means (including photocopying or storing it in any medium by electronic means and whether or not transiently or incidentally to some other use of this publication) without the written permission of the copyright owner, except in accordance with the provisions of the Copyright, Designs and Patents Act 1988 or under the terms of a licence issued by the Copyright Licensing Agency, 90 Tottenham Court Road, London W1T 4LP. Applications for the copyright owner's written permission should be addressed to the publisher.

Typeset by Thomson Digital, India

Original illustrations © Harcourt Education Limited, 2005

Cover design by Wooden Ark

Printed in UK by Bath Colour

Cover photo: © Getty Images

**Acknowledgements**
Every effort has been made to contact copyright holders of material reproduced in this book. Any omissions will be rectified in subsequent printings if notice is given to the publishers.

The author would like to express her deep gratitude and appreciation to Abdul Patel for working through the book several times and for his support, incredible patience and invaluable feedback during the writing of this book. A special thank you to Fayaz Roked and Fozia Roked for their help, encouragement and support. Thank you to Lewis Birchon, Gavin Fidler and Elaine Tuffery.

Microsoft product screenshots reprinted with permission from Microsoft Corporation.

# Contents

**UNIT 5: Create an e-presentation**

| | |
|---|---|
| Section 1: Create a master slide | 2 |
| Section 2: Enter data on slides and print slides | 28 |
| Section 3: Update a presentation | 44 |
| Quick reference – Create a master slide | 54 |
| Quick reference – Enter data on slides and print slides | 57 |
| Quick reference – Update a presentation | 59 |
| Build-up tasks | 61 |
| Practice tasks | 64 |
| Definition of terms | 67 |
| Preparation for the assessment | 69 |
| Index | 74 |

An introduction to the qualification and instructions for copying the resource files can be found on the accompanying CD-ROM.

# UNIT 5: Create an e-presentation

## How to use this book

This book is divided into three sections:

- in Section 1 you will learn how to create a master slide; how to format text sizes, font type and text emphasis; how to insert headers and footers; how to insert an image into the master slide; how to use a border; and how to save a presentation in a new folder

- in Section 2 you will learn how to enter titles and bulleted text on slides, how to promote and demote bulleted text and how to print individual slides, handouts and an Outline view

- in Section 3 you will learn how to make changes to a presentation – for example, how to insert, delete, and find and replace text; insert a new slide into an existing presentation; and create and fill a graphic shape.

You will use a software program called Microsoft Office PowerPoint 2003 which is part of Microsoft Office 2003. PowerPoint is a presentation program which allows you to create slides with images and drawings so that you can produce impressive presentations with ease. We will refer to it as PowerPoint from now on.

## How to work through this book

1. Before you begin this unit, make sure that you feel confident with the basics of using a computer and Windows XP. These skills are covered in Chapter 1 of the Unit 1 book *Learning to Pass New CLAiT: File management and e-document production*.

2. If there are some terms that you do not understand, refer to the Definition of terms on page 67.

3. Work through the book in sequence so that one skill is understood before moving on to the next. This ensures thorough understanding of the topic and prevents unnecessary mistakes.

4. Read the **>> How to...** guidelines which give step-by-step instructions for each skill; do not attempt to work through them. Read through the points and look at the screenshots – make sure that you understand all the instructions before moving on.

5. To make sure that you have understood how to perform a skill, work through the **Check your understanding** task that follows. You should refer to the How to… guidelines when doing the task.

6  At the end of each section is an **Assess your skills** table. This lists the skills that you will have practised by working through each section. Look at each item listed to help you decide whether you are confident that you can perform each skill.

7  Towards the end of this book are **Quick reference guides, Build-up** and **Practice tasks.** Work through each of the tasks.

If you need help, you may refer to the How to… guidelines or Quick reference guides whilst doing the build-up tasks. Whilst working on the Practice task you should feel confident enough to use only the Quick reference guides if you need support. These guides may also be used during an assessment.

Note: there are many ways of performing the skills covered in this book. However, this book provides guidelines that have proven to be easily understood by learners.

## Files for this book

To work through the tasks in this book, you will need the files from the folder called **files_presentations**. This folder is on the CD-ROM provided with this book. Copy this folder into your user area before you begin.

### ▶▶ How to... copy the folder **files_presentations** from the CD-ROM

Make sure the computer is switched on and the desktop screen is displayed.

1  Insert the CD-ROM into the CD-ROM drive of your computer.

2  Close any windows that may open.

3  From the desktop, double-click on the **My Computer** icon.

4  The **My Computer** window is displayed.

5  Under **Devices with Removable Storage**, double-click on the CD drive icon to view the contents of the CD-ROM.

6  A window will open displaying the contents of the CD-ROM.

7  Double-click on the folder **L1_Unit5_Presn**.

8  Click once on the folder **files_presentations**.

9  The folder will be highlighted, usually blue (Figure 1).

**FIGURE 1** The contents of the CD-ROM

Introduction  v

**10** In the **File and Folder Tasks** section, click on **Copy this folder**.

**11** The **Copy Items** dialogue box will be displayed (Figure 2).

**12** In this dialogue box, click on the user area where you want to copy the folder **files_presentations** to.

**13** Click on **Copy**. The folder **files_presentations** will be copied to your user area.

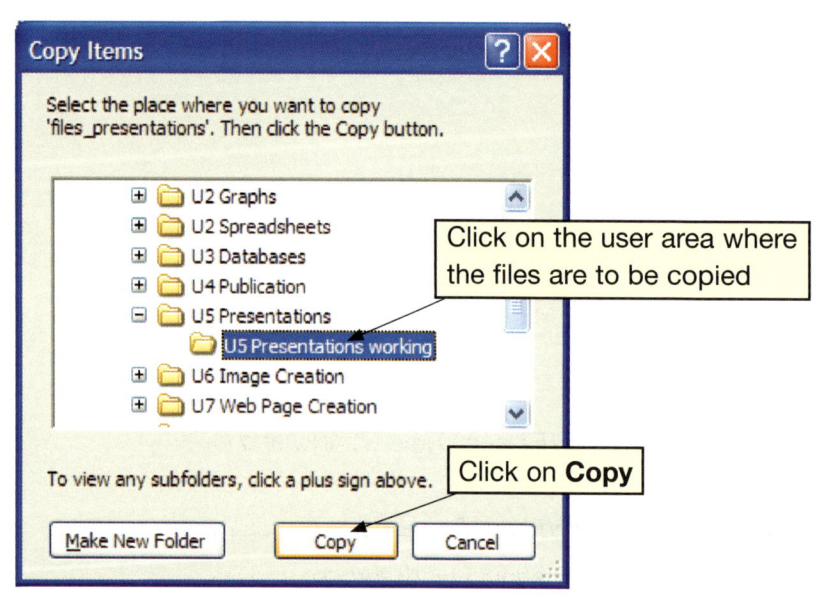

**FIGURE 2** The Copy Items dialogue box

For guidance on copying the resource files to your user area, please see the handout titled 'Preparing your work area' on the accompanying CD-ROM.

*Unit 5: Create an e-presentation*

## Who this book is suitable for

*Anyone working towards:*

- *OCR Level 1 Certificate or Diploma for IT Users (New CLAiT), and OCR ITQ qualification*
- *complete beginners, as no prior knowledge of PowerPoint is required*
- *use as a self-study workbook – the user should work through the book from start to finish*
- *tutor-assisted workshops or tutor-led groups*
- *individuals wanting to learn to use Microsoft Office PowerPoint 2003 (default settings are assumed).*

Although this book is based on PowerPoint 2003, it may also be suitable for users of PowerPoint 2002 (XP) and PowerPoint 2000. However, note that a few of the skills may be different and some screenshots will not be identical.

# UNIT 5: Create an e-presentation

## 1: Create a master slide

### LEARNING OUTCOMES

**In this section you will learn how to:**

- start PowerPoint
- understand the different parts of the PowerPoint screen
- go to Slide Master view
- understand and use the master slide layout (placeholders)
- set the slide orientation
- set the text style, size, alignment and emphasis for the title and bullets
- display a border
- set the border colour
- save a presentation into a new folder
- insert an image
- position an image
- resize an image
- move footer placeholders (frames)
- switch to Normal view to check the positioning of items
- format the background colour
- insert headers and footers into a master slide: name, centre number, automatic date, time, slide numbers
- use the different views in PowerPoint
- close a presentation
- exit PowerPoint.

## What is an e-presentation?

An e-presentation is an electronic presentation which displays a number of slides as a slide show. This presentation can be shown on screen or it can be printed out.

Presentations can be used for many purposes, for example, at conferences, to try to sell a product or service, or as a teaching aid. They can also be viewed in a variety of ways (e.g. on a computer screen, on a large screen using a data projector, copied on to overhead transparencies or printed out in a variety of formats to be given as handouts to an audience).

Presentation terms and actions will be explained throughout this book.

## Mouse techniques used in this book

The table below explains the different mouse techniques. Unless otherwise instructed, always click using the left mouse button.

| TECHNIQUE | ACTION |
| --- | --- |
| Point | Move the mouse on the mousemat until the pointer appears at the required position on the screen. |
| Click | Press and release the left mouse button once. |
| Double-click | Quickly press the left mouse button twice then release it. |
| Right-click | Press and release the right mouse button once – a menu displays. |
| Hover | Position the mouse pointer over an icon or menu item and pause, a Tool tip or a further menu will appear. |
| Click and drag | Used to move items. Click with the left mouse button on an item, hold the mouse button down and move the pointer to another location. Release the button. |

*Mouse techniques*

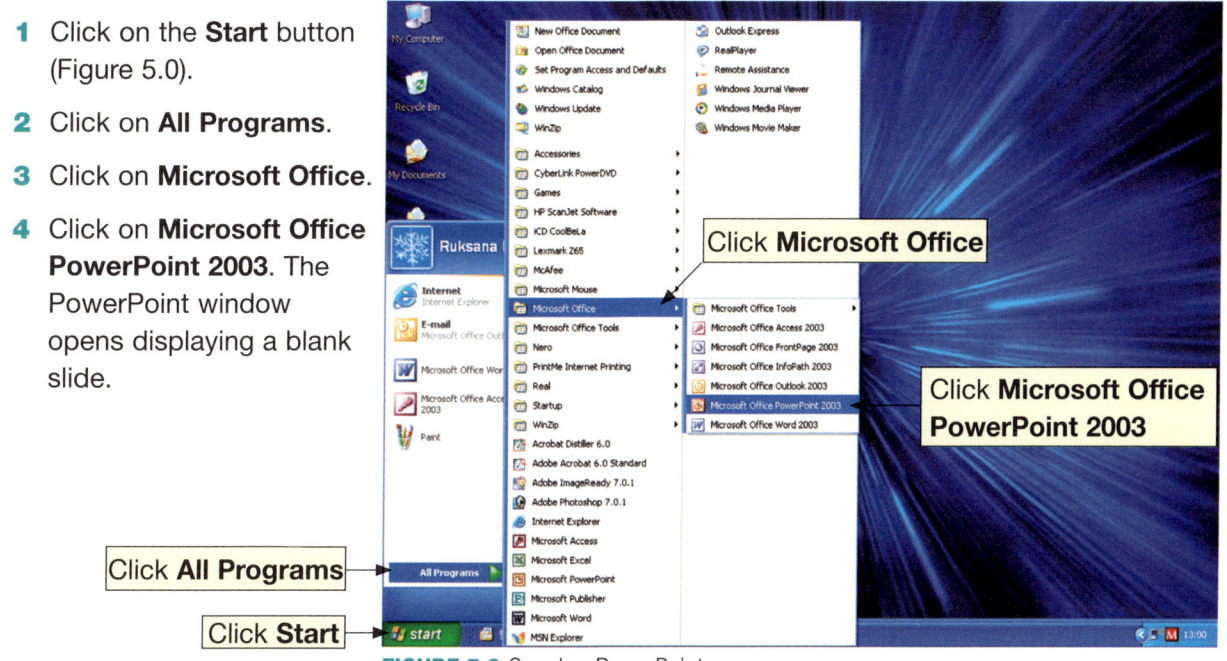

Switch on your computer and log in.

### ▶▶ How to... start PowerPoint

1 Click on the **Start** button (Figure 5.0).
2 Click on **All Programs**.
3 Click on **Microsoft Office**.
4 Click on **Microsoft Office PowerPoint 2003**. The PowerPoint window opens displaying a blank slide.

**FIGURE 5.0** Opening PowerPoint

Section 1: Create a master slide

> **Check your understanding** *Start PowerPoint*
>
> 1 Start PowerPoint.
>
> 2 A new presentation called **Presentation1** will open and a blank slide will be displayed.
>
> 3 Keep this open until you are instructed to close it.

## Getting familiar with the PowerPoint window

PowerPoint 2003 may open with the Task pane on the right (Figure 5.1). Click on the black cross next to **Getting Started** to close the task pane.

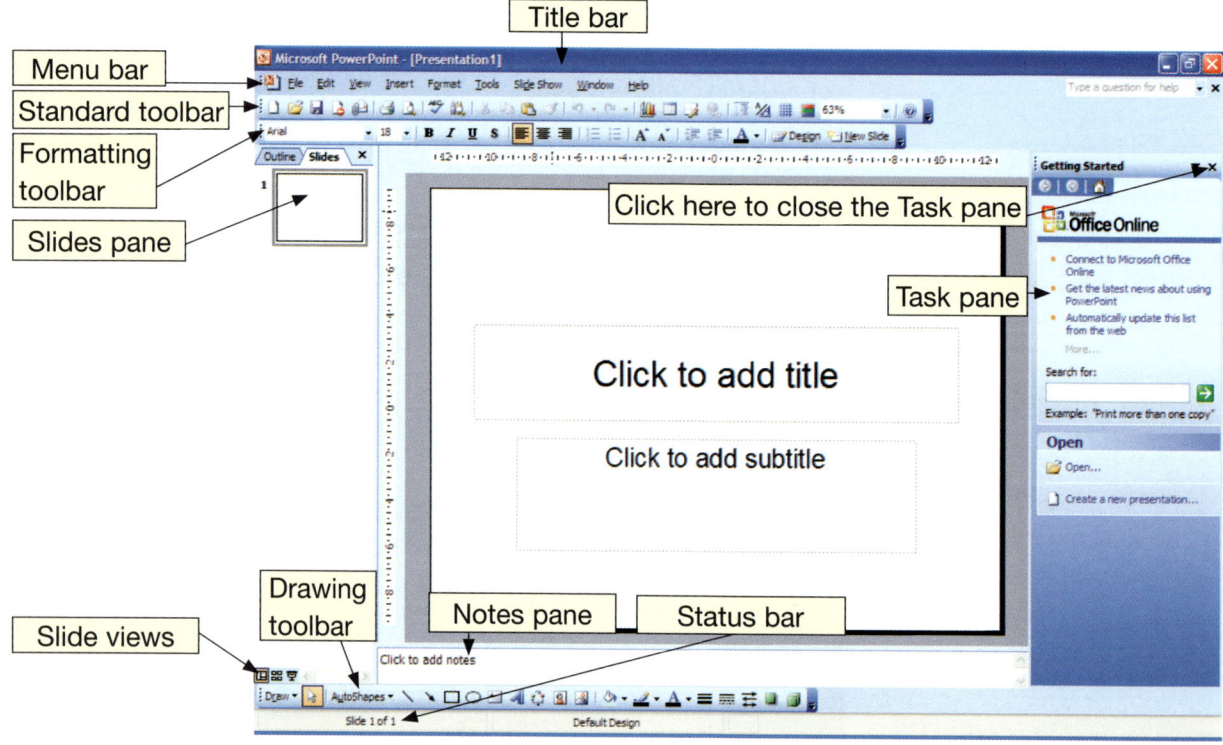

**FIGURE 5.1** The PowerPoint window

Take a few minutes to become familiar with the different parts of the PowerPoint window (see the table opposite).

Unit 5: Create an e-presentation

| PART OF WINDOW | DESCRIPTION |
| --- | --- |
| Title bar | Displays the title of the current presentation. |
| Menu bar | A list of options. Click on a menu item to see the drop-down menu. |
| Standard toolbar | Includes icons for commonly used tasks (e.g. Save, Print). |
| Formatting toolbar | Includes icons for commonly used formatting (e.g. bold, centre). |
| Slides pane | Displays two views:<br>● slides view displays a miniature of the slides (including images and headers and footers)<br>● outline view, which displays the slide text only. |
| Slide views | Display three different views of the presentation: Normal, Slide Sorter and Slide Show. |
| Drawing toolbar | Includes icons for common drawing items and autoshapes (e.g. arrows, callout boxes, etc.). |
| Status bar | Displays the number of the current slide and the total number of slides in a presentation. |
| Notes pane | Displays any speaker's notes. |

*The PowerPoint window*

If the Office Assistant (Figure 5.2) is visible on the screen, right-click on it. A menu will be displayed. Click on **Hide** from this menu to hide the Office Assistant on the screen.

### ▶▶ How to... use PowerPoint menus

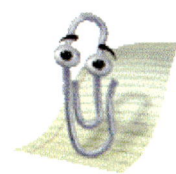

**FIGURE 5.2** The Office Assistant

1  In your PowerPoint window locate the Menu bar.
2  Click on **Format**.
3  A list will drop down with further choices.
4  At first the whole menu may not display, but if you leave it open for a few seconds it will display in full.
5  Another way to display the full menu is to click on the chevrons at the bottom of the menu ⌄ as soon as the menu drops down.
6  Click anywhere outside the menu or click on **Format** again to close the menu.

### Check your understanding  *Use menus*

Click on the **Format** menu. Look for:

1  the ghosted (greyed-out) options.
2  the picture buttons on the left of the menu which show the immediate action.
3  the options that will display a dialogue box (have three dots after the option).
4  the options that lead to a submenu (has an arrow on the right).

## The toolbar buttons

Move your mouse over each **toolbar** button and pause, a **Tool tip** will display showing the name of the button. Clicking on a toolbar button provides a quick way of carrying out tasks in a program. In this book, we will refer to a toolbar button as an icon.

> **What does it mean?**
> An icon is a button (picture) on the toolbar. The Save icon:

### Check your understanding — Use the icons on the toolbar

Move your mouse over the icons on the toolbar and pause on each button until the Tool tip displays.

## Making your PowerPoint window clearer

### The task pane

PowerPoint 2003 opens with the **task pane** on the right of the screen. You are advised to close the **task pane** so that the screen is clearer (optional).

You can click on the cross just above the task pane to close it every time you start PowerPoint, or you can set the option to close the task pane so that it does not display every time you start PowerPoint.

### ▶▶ How to... set the option to close the task pane (optional)

1. Click on the **Tools** menu.
2. Click on **Options**.
3. The **Options** dialogue box will be displayed.
4. Check the **View** tab is selected.
5. Click to remove the tick in the box for **Startup Task Pane**.
6. Click on **OK**.
7. The task pane will now not be displayed every time you start PowerPoint.

> **TIP!**
> Tabs look similar to section dividers in a filing cabinet. To select a tab, click on the tab name.

### Standard and Formatting toolbars

Are your Standard and Formatting toolbars on the same row? If so, it is helpful to display them on two rows so that you can see all the icons on both toolbars.

### ▶▶ How to... display the Standard and Formatting toolbars on two rows (optional)

1. Click on the **Toolbar Options** symbol, which is on the right end of the Standard toolbar.
2. A window will be displayed.

*Unit 5: Create an e-presentation*

**3** Click on **Show Buttons on Two Rows**.

**4** The Standard and Formatting toolbars will now be displayed on two rows.

## The keyboard and entering text

Entering text is also referred to as typing or keying in text. When you enter text, make sure you type the words exactly as shown. Use the same case as shown in the text you are copying (see table below).

| CASE | EXAMPLE |
| --- | --- |
| lower case | this text is in lower case – there are no capital letters. |
| Initial Capitals | Each Of These Words Has An Initial Capital. The First Letter Of Each Word Is A Capital. |
| UPPER CASE | THIS TEXT IS IN UPPER CASE. ALL THE LETTERS ARE CAPITAL LETTERS. |

*Examples of case*

When you enter text, make sure you use the correct spacing:

- Between each word: one space.
- At the end of a bulleted point press **Enter** once. There should not be a clear line space between bullets.

**▶▶ How to...** use the keyboard to enter data and to move around the screen

The following table explains the various ways you can use the keyboard to enter data and to move around the presentation.

| HOW TO | METHOD |
| --- | --- |
| See where text will be entered | Look for the flashing straight line on the screen. Your text will be entered wherever this line is. This is called the cursor (or I-beam). |
| Type one capital letter | Hold down the Shift key and press the required letter on the keyboard. Then let go of the Shift key. |
| Type word(s) in capital letters | Press down the Caps Lock key. |
| Type lower case letters | Check that Caps Lock is switched off. |
| Insert a space between words | Press the spacebar once. |
| Delete a letter to the left of the cursor | Press the Backspace key. |
| Delete a letter to the right of the cursor | Press the Delete key. |
| Move to the next line | Press the Enter key. |
| Move to the beginning of the line | Press the Home key. |
| Move to the end of the line | Press the End key. |

(continued overleaf)

| HOW TO | METHOD |
| --- | --- |
| Move to the beginning of the presentation | Press the Ctrl and Home keys at the same time. |
| Move to the end of the presentation | Press the Ctrl and End keys at the same time. |
| Move to the next slide | Press the Page Down key. |
| Move to the previous slide | Press the Page Up key. |

*Entering data and moving around the presentation using the keyboard*

## Master slides

A *master slide* is used to make sure that all the slides in a presentation have a consistent layout. For example:

- a company logo would usually be displayed in the same place and in the same size on all slides
- the font type, size and alignment on all slides should be consistent
- the background colour on all slides should be the same
- headers and footers on all slides should be the same size and in the same place.

PowerPoint has a Slide Master feature which enables you to ensure that all items in a presentation are displayed and formatted consistently. Therefore it is important to make sure that you set up the master slide correctly as it usually forms the basis on which all the slides in a presentation are created.

### ▶▶ How to... create a master slide

1 Click on the **View** menu.

2 Click on **Master**, then on **Slide Master** (Figure 5.3).

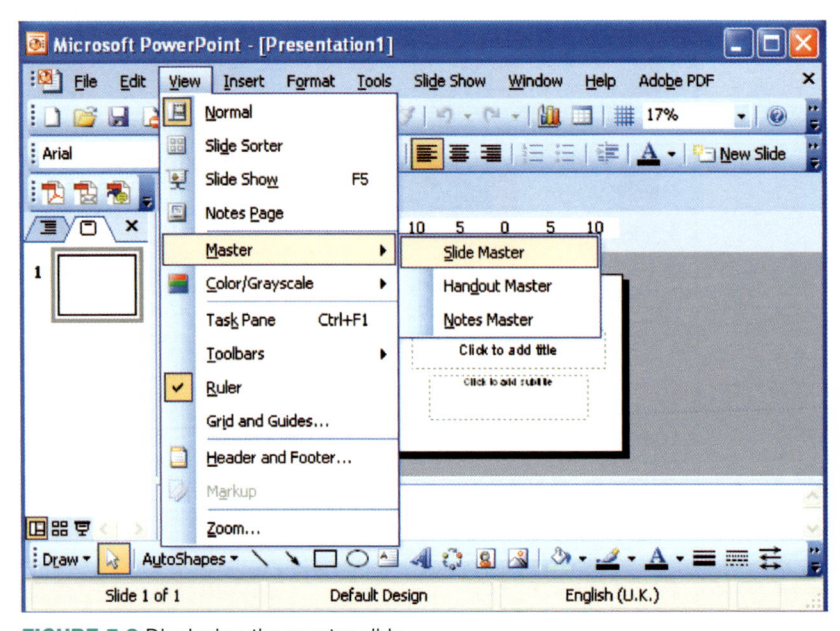

**FIGURE 5.3** Displaying the master slide

**3** The master slide will be displayed.

**4** The frames (boxes) displayed on the master slide are referred to as *placeholders*.

> **Check your understanding** *Create a master slide*
>
> In your **Presentation1**, go to the Slide Master.

## Getting familiar with the Master Slide view

Take a few minutes to become familiar with the different parts of the Master Slide view (Figure 5.4).

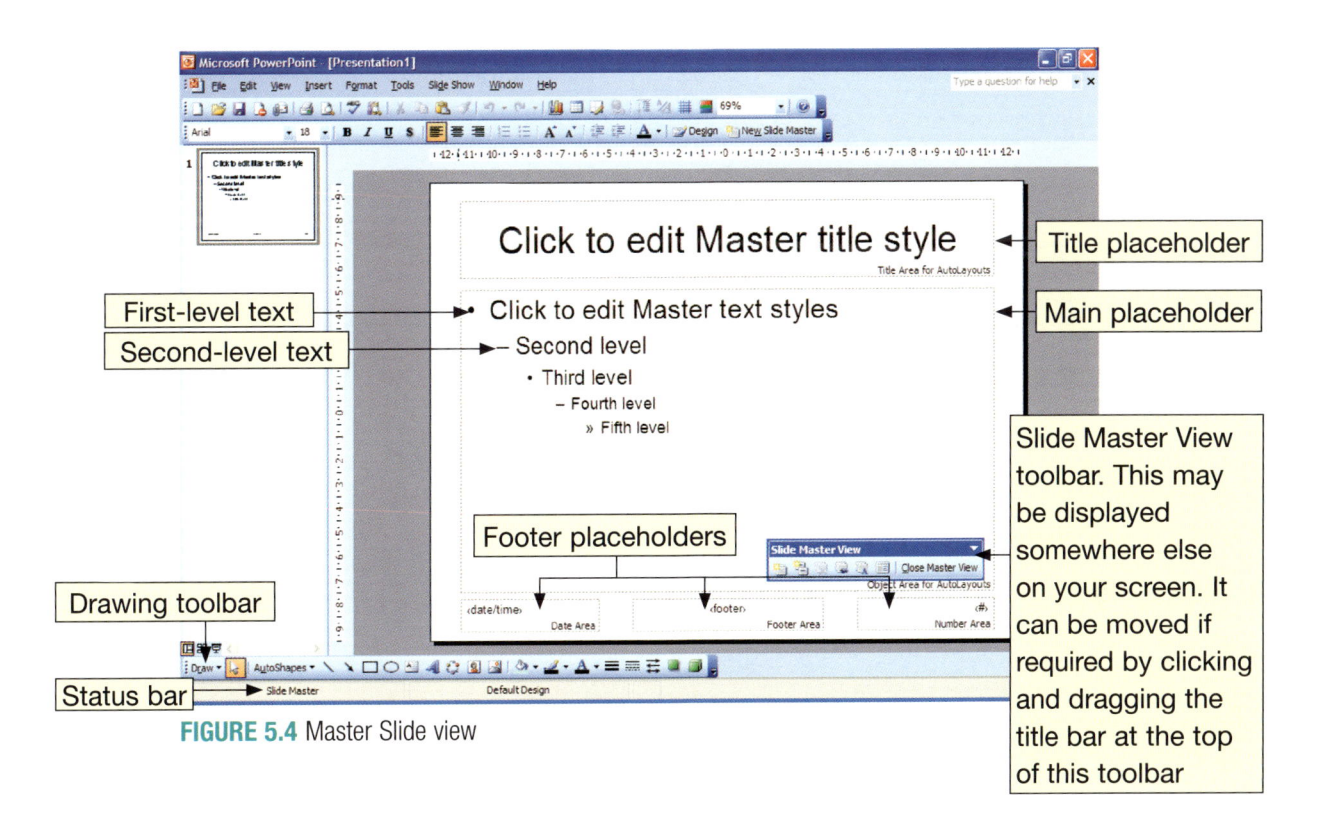

**FIGURE 5.4** Master Slide view

Bullets are used to emphasise points in a slide. Any style of bullet character can be used, however, you are advised not to change the default styles displayed by PowerPoint.

Look at the main placeholder (frame) on your screen. The bullet character for the first level of text **Click to edit Master text styles** is a round dot. The bullet character for the second level of text **Second level** is a dash. Ignore the other text levels because you will only use the first and second levels. You may delete the third, fourth and fifth levels if you wish.

Section 1: Create a master slide

### Check your understanding  *Slide Master view*

1 Click with your mouse in the title placeholder (frame).
  Note how the border of the surrounding box changes and the text **Click to edit Master title style** becomes highlighted.

2 Click with your mouse in the first line of the text **Click to edit Master text styles** in the main placeholder (frame).
  Note how the border of the surrounding box changes and the text **Click to edit Master text styles** becomes highlighted.

3 Click with your mouse in the second line of text **Second level** in the main placeholder (frame). Note how the text **Second level** becomes highlighted.

## Slide orientation

Slide orientation refers to the way in which the slide is displayed:

- Portrait: the shortest sides are at the top and bottom.
- Landscape: the longest sides are at the top and bottom.

The default orientation of slides in PowerPoint is landscape.

### ▶▶ How to... *set the slide orientation*

1 Click on the **File menu**.
2 Click on **Page Setup**.
3 The **Page Setup** dialogue box will be displayed (Figure 5.5).
4 In the Slides section, click on **Portrait** or **Landscape**.
5 Click on **OK**.

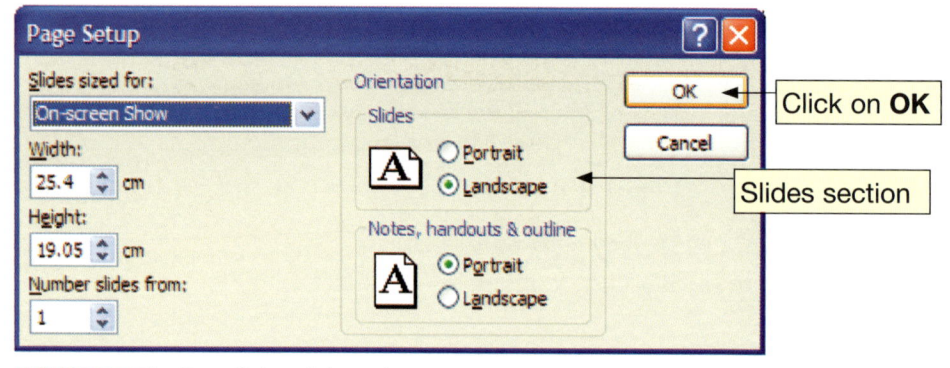

**FIGURE 5.5** The Page Setup dialogue box

### Check your understanding  *Set the slide orientation*

In your **Presentation1**, set the slide orientation to **landscape**.

Unit 5: Create an e-presentation

# Setting up text styles on the master slide

You will need to set the text emphasis and the alignment for the heading, the first-level bullet and the second-level bullet (sub-bullet). You may also need to display a border.

PowerPoint automatically sets a large font size for the title, a medium size for the first-level bullet and a smaller size for the second-level bullet. Therefore you may not need to change the size of these if exact font sizes are not specified.

PowerPoint automatically sets bullet characters for each of the text levels in the main placeholder. Therefore you do not have to apply bullet characters. The second-level bullet is automatically indented from the first-level bullet so you do not have to set an indent.

## Text enhancement

Text enhancement is also referred to as emphasis. Emphasis is used to make text stand out. Text can be emphasised using **bold**, *italic* or underline.

## Alignment

Alignment is how the text lines up with the left and right side of the placeholder on the slide. In PowerPoint, you can align text to the left, centre or right.

**▶▶ How to...** set the style for the title

1. Before you can set the style for the title you must first select it.

2. Click anywhere in the text **Click to edit Master title style**.

3. The text will now be highlighted (Figure 5.6).

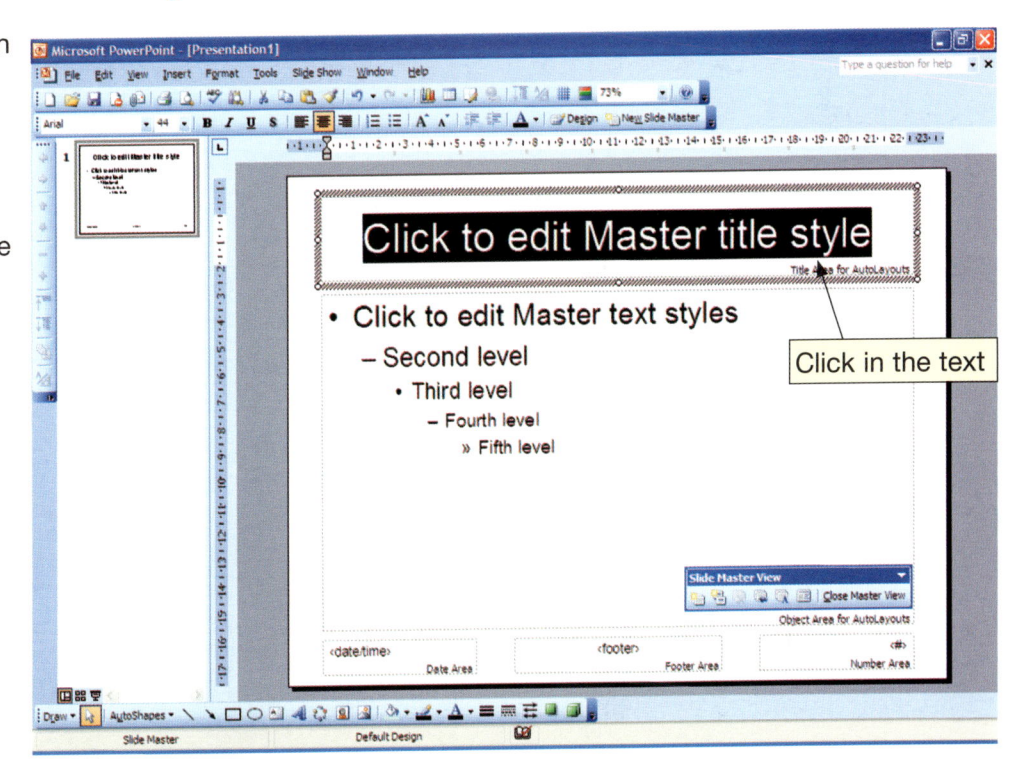

**FIGURE 5.6** Selecting the title

### ▶▶ How to... set the emphasis for the title

1 On the **Formatting** toolbar, click on the icon(s) **B** *I* <u>U</u> for the required emphasis (bold, italic or underline).

### ▶▶ How to... set the size for the title

1 On the **Formatting** toolbar, click on the **drop-down arrow** to the right of the **Font Size** box 44.

2 From the drop-down list click on the required size.

> **TIP!**
> Remember, you may not need to change the default font size set by PowerPoint.

### ▶▶ How to... set the alignment for the title

1 On the **Formatting** toolbar, click on the icon for the required alignment (left, centre or right).

2 The text style for the title should now be set.

---

**Check your understanding**  **Set the title text style**

In your **Presentation1**, set up the text style as follows:

| STYLE | EMPHASIS | SIZE | ALIGNMENT |
|-------|----------|------|-----------|
| title | bold only | large | centre |

---

### ▶▶ How to... set the style for the first-level text

1 In the main placeholder (frame), click anywhere within the text **Click to edit Master text styles**.

2 The text will now be highlighted (Figure 5.7).

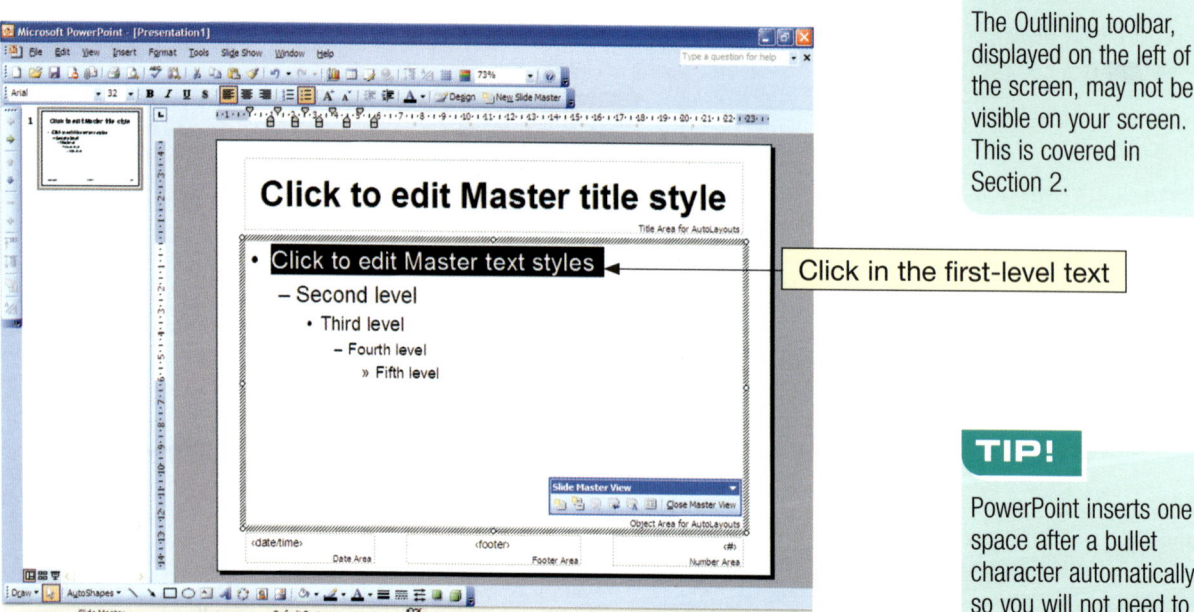

> **TIP!**
> The Outlining toolbar, displayed on the left of the screen, may not be visible on your screen. This is covered in Section 2.

**FIGURE 5.7** Selecting first-level text

> **TIP!**
> PowerPoint inserts one space after a bullet character automatically so you will not need to change the spacing.

Unit 5: Create an e-presentation

## How to... set the emphasis for the first-level text

1. On the **Formatting** toolbar, click on the icon(s) **B** *I* <u>U</u> for the required emphasis (bold, italic or underline).

## How to... set the size for the first-level text

1. On the **Formatting** toolbar, click on the **drop-down arrow** to the right of the **Font Size** box.
2. From the drop-down list, click on a font size that is smaller than the title.

> **TIP!**
> Remember, you do not need to change the default font size set by PowerPoint.

## How to... set the alignment for the first-level text

1. On the **Formatting** toolbar, click on the icon for the required alignment (left, centre or right).
2. The text style for the first-level bullet in the main placeholder should now be set.

### Check your understanding — Set the first-level text style

In your **Presentation1**, set up the text style as follows:

| STYLE | EMPHASIS | SIZE | ALIGNMENT |
| --- | --- | --- | --- |
| first-level text | none | medium | left |

## How to... set the style for the second-level text

1. In the main placeholder (frame), click anywhere within the text **Second level**.
2. The text will now be highlighted (Figure 5.8).

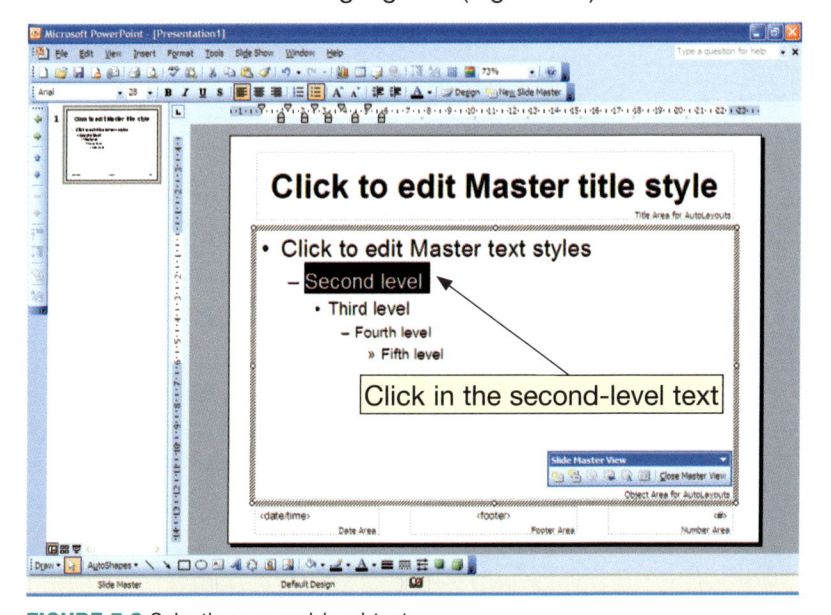

**FIGURE 5.8** Selecting second-level text

> **TIP!**
> Avoid changing the default bullet character styles, as some bullet character styles do not display the space after the bullet clearly.

Section 1: Create a master slide    13

## ▶▶ How to... set the emphasis for the second-level text

On the **Formatting** toolbar, click on the icon(s) **B** *I* U for the required emphasis (bold, italic or underline).

## ▶▶ How to... set the size for the second-level text

1. On the **Formatting** toolbar, click on the **drop-down arrow** to the right of the **Font Size** box.
2. From the drop-down list, click on a font size that is smaller than the first-level text.

> **TIP!**
> Remember, you may not need to change the default font size set by PowerPoint.

## ▶▶ How to... set the alignment for the second-level text

1. On the **Formatting** toolbar, click on the icon for the required alignment (left, centre or right).
2. The text style for the second-level bullet in the main placeholder should now be set.

### Check your understanding  Set the second-level text style

In your **Presentation1**, set up the text style as follows:

| STYLE | EMPHASIS | SIZE | ALIGNMENT |
|---|---|---|---|
| second-level text | italic only | small | left and indented from first-level bullet |

# Lines and borders (boxes)

Lines and borders (boxes) are used around a placeholder or an image to make it stand out.

Lines and borders can be displayed on the slide master or in Normal view on individual slides.

There are several ways to draw borders. The quickest method is to use the Drawing toolbar. Look at the bottom left of your screen: is the Drawing toolbar displayed (Figure 5.9)?

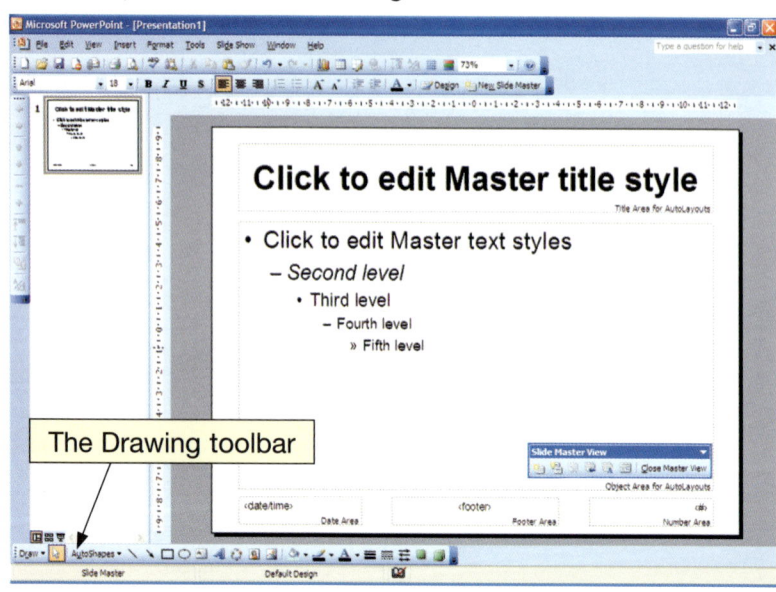

**FIGURE 5.9** The Drawing toolbar

Unit 5: Create an e-presentation

## How to... display the Drawing toolbar

1 Click on the **View** menu.
2 Click on **Toolbars**.
3 If there is no tick in front of **Drawing**, click on **Drawing**.
4 The Drawing toolbar will be displayed at the bottom of the screen.

## How to... display a border

1 Click in the placeholder (frame) for which you want to create a border OR click once on an image to select it.
2 On the Drawing toolbar, click on the **Line Style** icon ≡ (Figure 5.10) or the **Dash Style** icon.
3 A selection of available styles will be displayed.

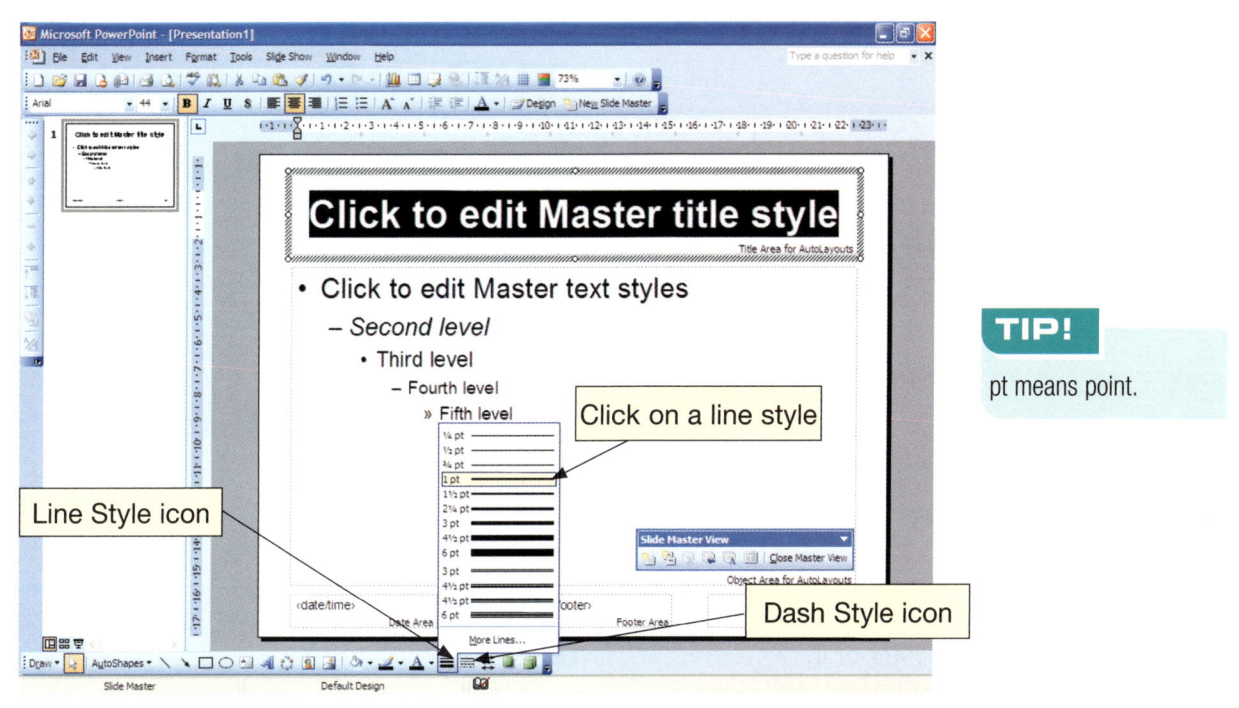

**FIGURE 5.10** The Line Style icon

> **TIP!**
> pt means point.

4 Click on a suitable line style (one that is not too thick or too thin, which would be difficult to see on a printout).
5 A border will be displayed around the placeholder or image.

> **TIP!**
> Choose a line of at least 1 pt.

## How to... set the border colour

1 Click anywhere in the placeholder or click on the image for which you have created a border.

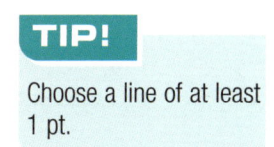

2 On the Drawing toolbar, click on the **drop-down arrow** next to the **Line Color** icon. A window will open displaying various colours (Figure 5.11).

3 Click on one of the colour squares.

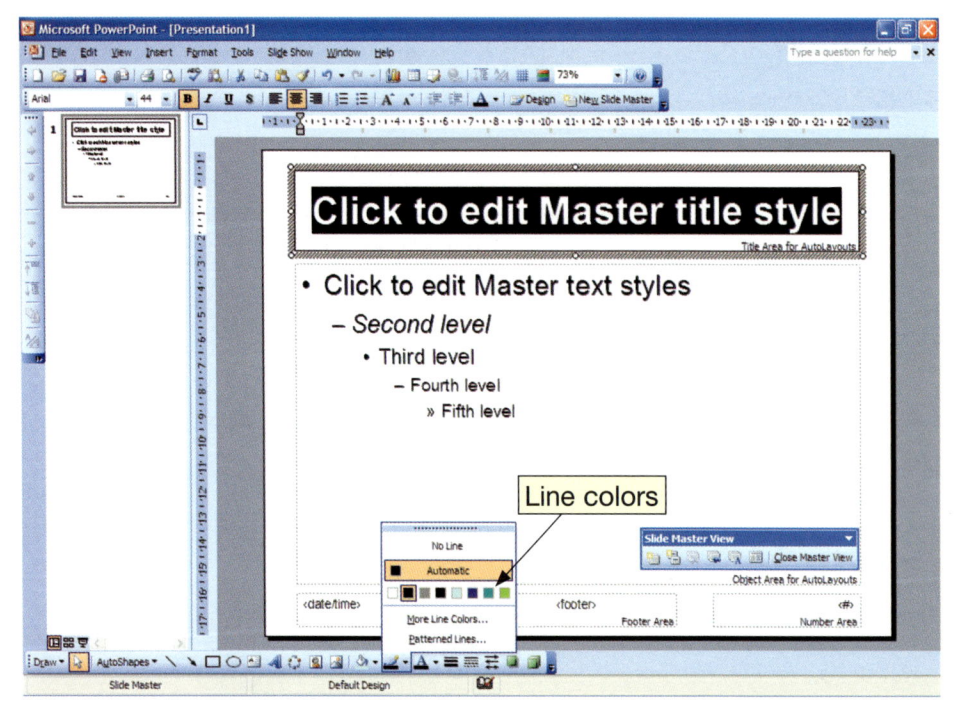

**FIGURE 5.11** Line colours

**TIP!**
Use black as this will display more clearly on a printout.

## Check your understanding  Insert a border

1 In your **Presentation1**, create a border of **1 pt** for the title placeholder.

2 Make sure the border colour is **black**.

## Saving your presentation

**How to...** save a presentation in a new folder in PowerPoint

1 Click on the **File** menu.

2 Click on **Save As**.

3 The **Save As** dialogue box will be displayed.

4 Click on the down arrow to the right of the **Save in** box. A list of user areas will be displayed.

**TIP!**
It is good practice to save your files into folders in your working area to keep your files organised.

Unit 5: Create an e-presentation

5. Click on your user area. The folder/user area name will be displayed in the **Save in** box (Figure 5.12).

6. Double-click to open the folders or subfolders in your user area.

7. Click on the **Create New Folder** icon.

8. The **New Folder** dialogue box will be displayed (Figure 5.13).

9. Enter the new folder name.

10. Click on **OK**.

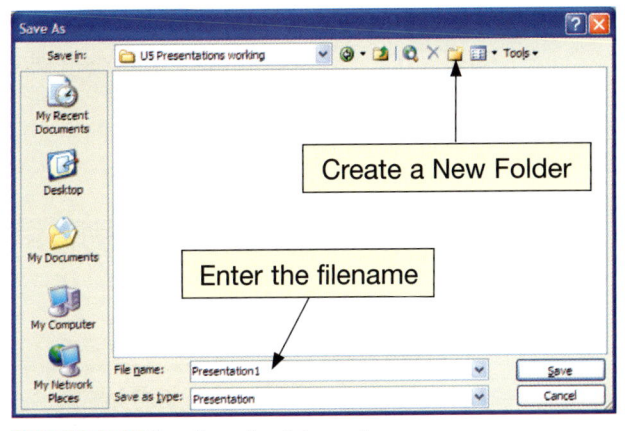

**FIGURE 5.12** The Save As dialogue box

**FIGURE 5.13** The New Folder box

**TIP!**
Do not enter a full stop after a file or folder name.

11. In the **Save As** dialogue box, in the **File name** box, delete any existing text.

12. Type in the required filename.

13. In the **Save as type** box, make sure **Presentation** is displayed.

14. Click on the **Save** button.

15. Your presentation will be saved in a new folder in your user area.

**▶▶ How to...** *save an existing presentation*

Click the **Save** icon on the Standard toolbar OR click on the **File** menu then click on **Save**.

**Check your understanding** *Save your presentation*

Save your **Presentation1** using the filename **trips** in a folder called **cyu tasks** in your user area.

## Inserting an image (graphic) into a master slide

You will need to learn how to insert an image into a master slide and into a particular slide in a presentation.

An image inserted into a master slide will be displayed on all the slides in a presentation. It is therefore important that the image is sized correctly and is placed in the correct position so that it will not touch or overlap the text (when text is entered) on any of the slides in the presentation.

Section 1: Create a master slide  17

## ▶▶ How to... *insert an image*

To insert an image on a master slide, make sure you are in Slide Master view. To insert an image on an individual slide, make sure you are in Normal view and that the slide on which you want to insert the image is selected.

1. Click on the **Insert** menu.
2. Click on **Picture**.
3. Click on **From File** (Figure 5.14).

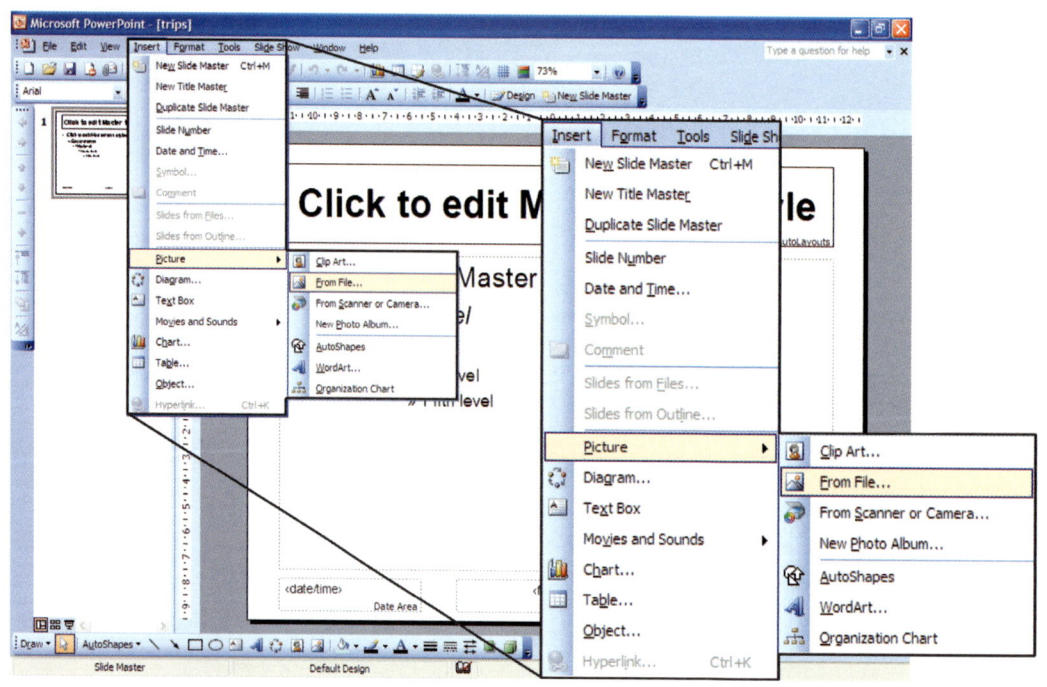

**FIGURE 5.14** Inserting a picture on the master slide

4. The **Insert Picture** dialogue box will be displayed (Figure 5.15).
5. Click on the **drop-down arrow** next to the **Look in** box.
6. Go to the user area (folder) in which the image is saved.
7. Check that **All pictures** is displayed next to the **Files of type** box.
8. Click on the image to be inserted. The image name and icon will be highlighted.
9. Click on **Insert**.
10. The image will be inserted on to the slide.

**FIGURE 5.15** The Insert Picture dialogue box

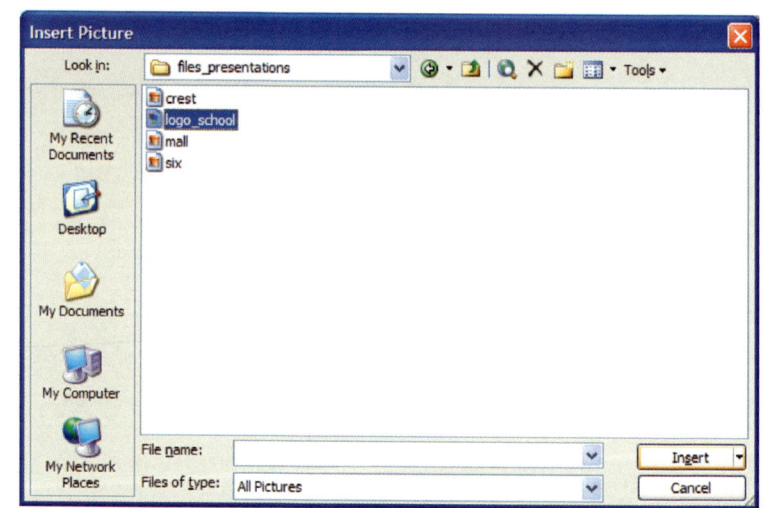

Unit 5: Create an e-presentation

Look at your screen (Figure 5.16) – round handles are displayed around the picture and a Picture toolbar may display somewhere on the screen.

**TIP!**

Do not worry if the image is too big or too small and if it is in the wrong place, you will learn how to resize the image and how to position it correctly.

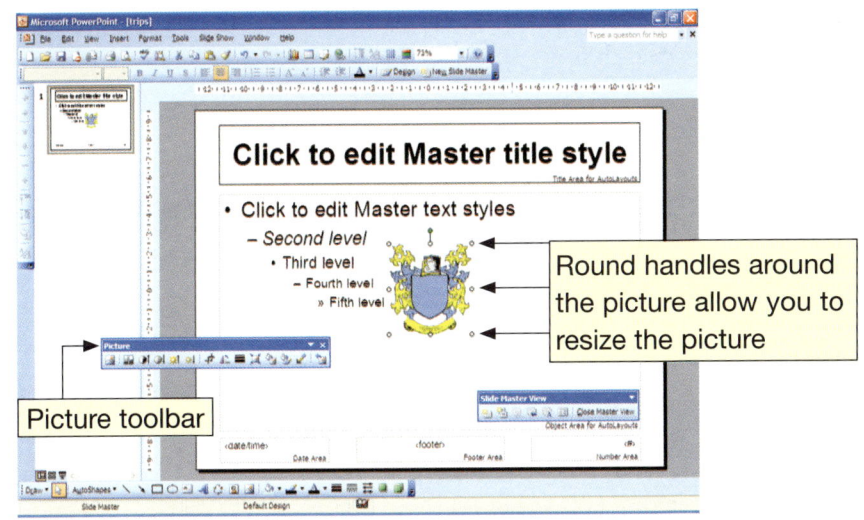

**FIGURE 5.16** Inserting an image into the master slide

## Check your understanding  *Insert an image into the master slide*

1. In your presentation **trips**, insert the image **logo_school** into the master slide.
2. Do not move the image yet – you will learn how to position it correctly later.
3. Save your presentation keeping the filename **trips**.

### ▶▶ How to...  *position an image*

1. Check to see if the round handles are displayed around the image.
2. If not, click on the image – the handles will be displayed.
3. Position your mouse anywhere within the image.
4. The mouse pointer will change to a four-headed arrow ✥.
5. Click and drag the image to the required position.
6. Make sure that no parts of the image or round handles extend into the grey area outside the master slide (Figure 5.17).

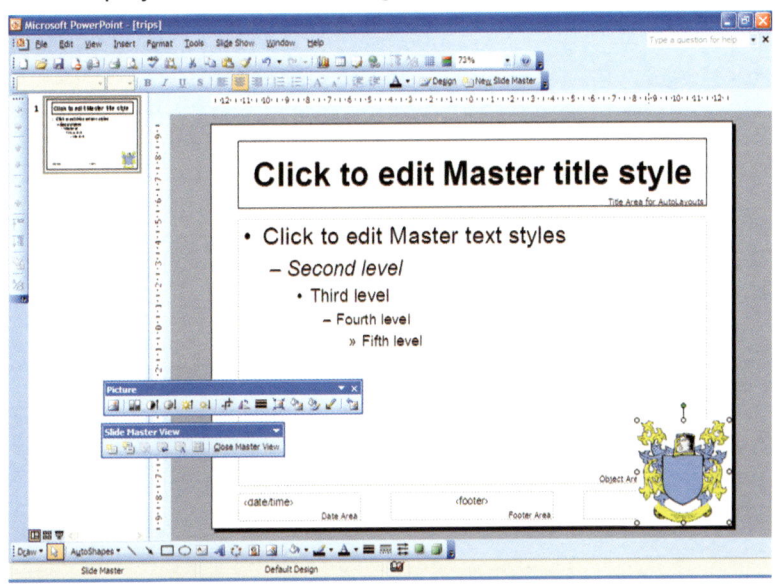

**FIGURE 5.17** Positioning an image on the master slide

Section 1: Create a master slide  19

7 Do not worry that the image overlaps (is on top of) other placeholders, you will learn how to move placeholders (frames) later.

> **Check your understanding** *Position an image on the master slide*
>
> 1 In your presentation **trips**, move the image **logo_school** to the bottom right corner of the slide.
> 2 Make sure the image remains in the white slide area and that no part of the image or handles extends into the grey area outside the slide.
> 3 Save your presentation keeping the filename **trips**.

## ▶▶ How to... *resize an image*

1 Position your mouse on a *corner* handle of the image.
2 The mouse will turn into a diagonal double-headed arrow ↖ (Figure 5.18).
3 To reduce the image size, click and drag the double-headed arrow inwards.
4 To increase the image size, click and drag the double-headed arrow outwards.

**TIP!**

Do not position your mouse on the centre handles – dragging on the centre handles will distort the image (change its shape).

**TIP!**

Refer to these guidelines to position or resize drawn shapes.

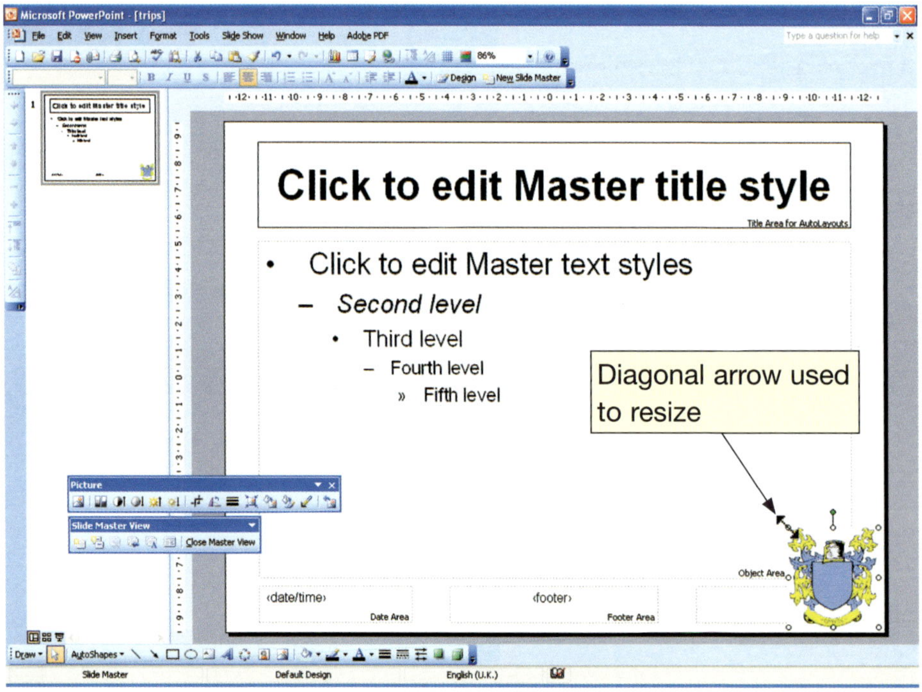

**FIGURE 5.18** The diagonal double-headed arrow used to resize an image

Unit 5: Create an e-presentation

### Check your understanding — *Position an image on the master slide*

1 In your presentation **trips**, resize the image **logo_school** so that it is visibly smaller than it was originally.

2 Make sure that you do not distort the image.

3 Save the presentaton.

## Positioning of images and text

If you have placed an image at the bottom left, right or centre of the master slide it may overlap with the footer placeholders. You should move the placeholders so that text and images do not overlap. It does not matter if the placeholder borders touch or overlap because the borders do not display on a printout.

**TIP!**

Do not click and drag the frame to the required position – you have more precise control using the keyboard.

### ▶▶ How to... *move placeholders*

1 Click on the placeholder (frame). Round handles display around it.

2 Find the **Ctrl** key on the keyboard.

3 Find the **cursor** keys (arrow keys) and locate the cursor key pointing in the direction in which you want to move the frame.

4 Hold down both the **Ctrl** key and the **cursor** key at the same time.

5 Tap the cursor key until the placeholder is moved to the required position.

6 Repeat this process to move any other placeholders (Figure 5.19).

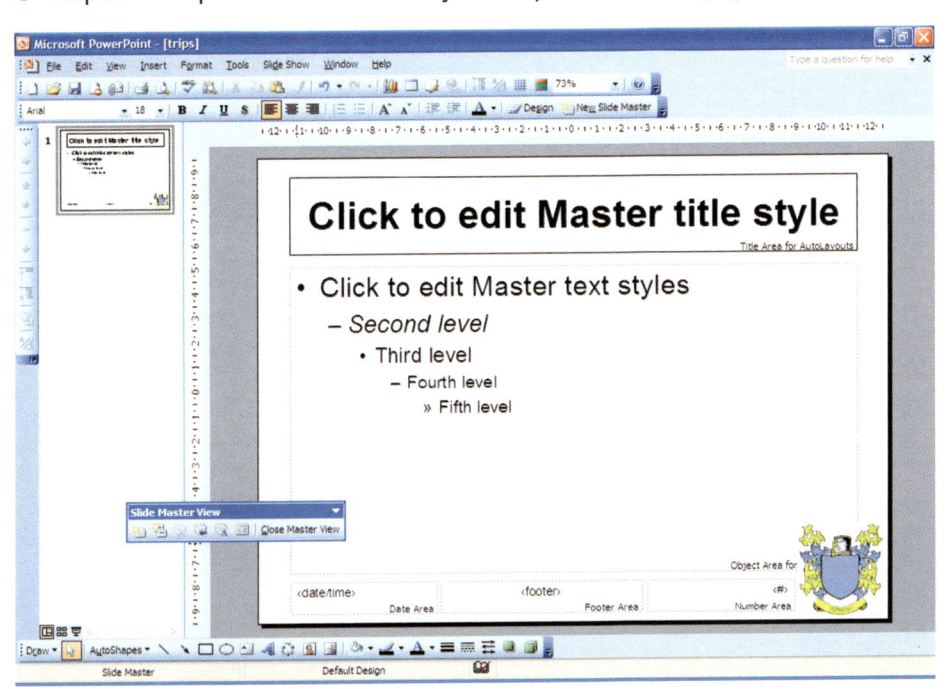

**FIGURE 5.19** Moving placeholders

Section 1: Create a master slide

### Check your understanding  Move the footer placeholders

1. In your presentation **trips**, move the **Footer Area** placeholder further to the left, towards the **Date Area** placeholder.
2. Move the **Number Area** placeholder further to the left, towards the **Footer Area** placeholder.
3. Save the presentation keeping the filename **trips**.

### ▶▶ How to... check the positioning of items in Normal view

When you have positioned and resized an image, you should switch to Normal slide view to make sure that all items are placed correctly and do not touch or overlap.

1. Click on the **View** menu.
2. Click **Normal**.

*In Normal view:*

The image and any footer items that you may have inserted will be displayed on the slide. If any items are not placed correctly, make a note of this.

*To return to the master slide:*

1. Click on the **View** menu.
2. Click on **Master**.
3. Click on **Slide Master**.

**TIP!**

A quick way to go to Normal view is to click the button **Close Master View** on the Slide Master View toolbar (Figure 5.20).

Click here to close the master slide

**FIGURE 5.20** The Close Master View button

### Check your understanding
### Check the position of the logo in Slide view

1. View your presentation **trips** in Normal view.
2. Check the position of the image.
3. Note that the footer placeholders will not yet display because you have not inserted any headers and footers.
4. Switch back to the Slide Master.

Unit 5: Create an e-presentation

# Applying a background consistently

Usually, the same background will be displayed on all the slides in a presentation. Any background that is set should be displayed consistently (the same) on all the slides. To ensure consistency, the background should be set on the master slide instead of on individual slides.

Often a background is set to white because this saves on printer ink (toner) when the presentation is printed and can make the presentation clearer to read on the screen.

### ▶▶ How to... *format the background on a master slide*

1. Click on the **Format** menu.
2. Click on **Background**.
3. The **Background** dialogue box will be displayed (Figure 5.21).
4. Click on the **drop-down arrow** next to the sample colour displayed (usually white).
5. A selection of colours will be displayed.
6. Click on a colour box to select a colour.
7. Click on **Apply to All**.
8. The background colour will be displayed on all the slides in the presentation (unless the colour selected was white).

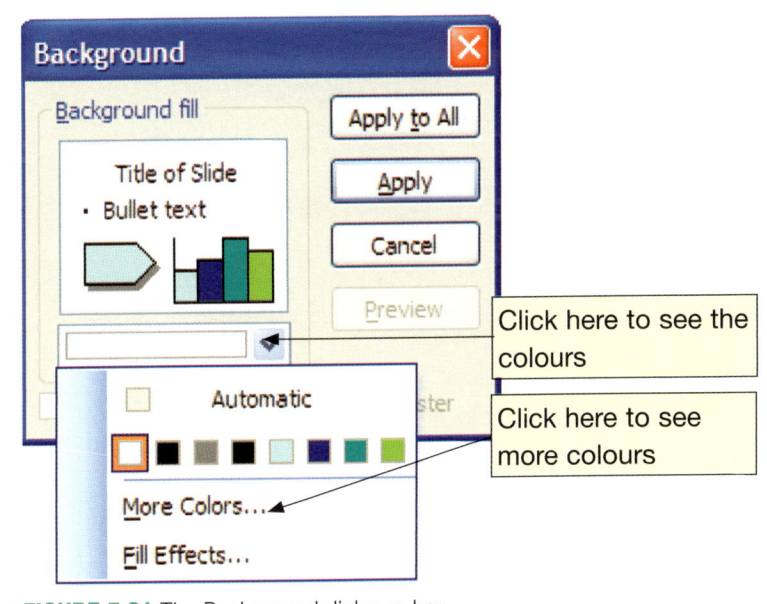

**FIGURE 5.21** The Background dialogue box

### Check your understanding — *Format the background*

1. In your presentation **trips**, format the background to white.
2. Save the presentation keeping the filename **trips**.

## Headers and footers

On a master slide in PowerPoint there are some default footer placeholders. The date and footer text can be entered into these placeholders or, alternatively, header and footer text can be entered using menus. You will learn how to insert headers and footers using menus.

The default placeholders can be moved to other parts of the master slide before or after you insert headers and footers.

## ▶▶ How to... display headers and footers on a master slide

If you need to insert your name and centre number, an automatic date (and time) and slide numbers on the master slide, you can insert all these items in the Header and Footer dialogue box.

1 Click on the **View** menu.
2 Click on **Header and Footer**.
3 The **Header and Footer** dialogue box will be displayed (Figure 5.22).
4 Click to place a tick in the box for **Date and time**.
5 Click in the button **Update automatically**.

*To insert an automatic date and the time:*

- Click on the drop-down arrow next to the date (Figure 5.23). A list of date and time formats will be displayed.
- Click on an option that displays the date and the time.

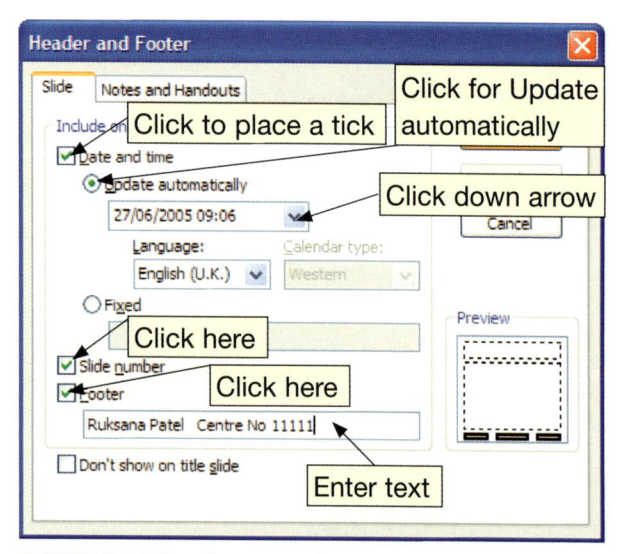

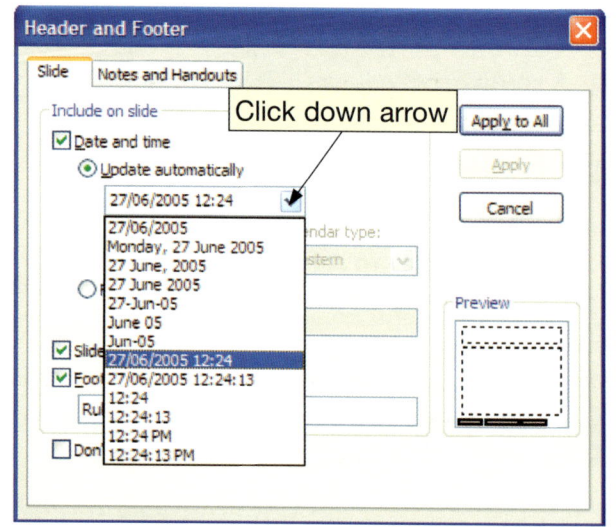

**FIGURE 5.22** The Header and Footer dialogue box

**FIGURE 5.23** Selecting the date and the time

6 In the **Language** box, click on the down arrow and select **English (U.K.)**.
7 Click to place a tick in the box **Slide number**.
8 Click to place a tick in the box for **Footer** and enter your name and centre number in the box below **Footer**.
9 Click on **Apply to All**.

*On the master slide:*

- in the <date/time> placeholder the actual date will not display
- in the <footer> placeholder the footer text you entered will not display

Unit 5: Create an e-presentation

- in the Number Area placeholder <#> will display instead of a number

Do not worry, the headers and footers will display in Normal view.

> **How to...** check headers and footers in Normal view

1 Click on the **View** menu, click on **Normal** OR click **Close Master view** on the **Slide Master toolbar**.

2 Check that the headers and footers are displayed correctly on the slide.

3 To return to the master slide, click on the **View** menu, click **Master**, click **Slide Master**.

### Check your understanding  Insert headers and footers

1 In your presentation **trips**, use the **View** menu and enter the following **footers**:
   - your **name** and **centre number**
   - an **automatic date** and the **time**.

2 Display the **slide number**.

3 Make sure the contents of the footer area do not touch or overlap the image.

4 Switch to Normal view to check that all items on your master slide are positioned correctly. Switch back to Slide Master view.

5 Save your presentation keeping the filename **trips**.

## Learning about the different views in PowerPoint

In PowerPoint there are different ways to view a presentation on screen. Each view shows the slides in the presentation in a different way (see table below). The view buttons are displayed at the bottom left of the screen, above the Drawing toolbar.

| VIEW | ICON | EXPLANATION |
| --- | --- | --- |
| Normal |  | This view shows the slide in the main area, with the Notes pane below the slide and the Slides pane (or the Outline pane) on the left. |
|  |  | You are advised to keep the view in Normal. Clicking and dragging the dividing bar can resize the Notes pane and the Slides section. |
| Slide Sorter |  | This view shows a miniature of all the slides in a presentation. Slide Sorter view can be used to check the number and the order of slides and to move slides. |
| Slide Show from current slide |  | This is the view used to run the presentation, usually for an audience. |

*The different views in PowerPoint*

### Check your understanding
### Use the different views in PowerPoint

1 Look at the bottom left of the PowerPoint screen above the Drawing toolbar.
2 Hover your mouse over the **Normal** view icon.
3 Click on the icon for **Slide Sorter View**, a miniature of your slide will be displayed.
4 Click on the icon for **Slide Show from current slide**. Your slide will be run as a presentation.
5 Click in your slide once. A blank screen will be displayed with the words **End of slide show, click to exit**.
6 Click this once, then click on the **Normal view** icon to return to Normal view.
7 Save your presentation keeping the filename **trips**.

## Closing a presentation

**How to...** close a presentation

1 Click on the **File** menu.
2 Click on **Close**.

## Exiting PowerPoint

**How to...** exit PowerPoint

1 Click on the **File** menu.
2 Click on **Exit**.

### Check your understanding
### Close a presentation and exit PowerPoint

1 Close your presentation **trips**.
2 Exit PowerPoint.

# ASSESS YOUR SKILLS – Create a master slide

By working through Section 1 you will have learnt the skills below. Read each item to help you decide how confident you feel about each skill.

- start PowerPoint
- recognise the different parts of the PowerPoint screen
- go to Slide Master view
- use the master slide layout (placeholders)
- set the slide orientation
- set the text style, size, alignment and emphasis for the title
- set the text style, size, alignment and emphasis for the first and second-level bullets
- display a border
- set the border colour
- save a presentation into a new folder
- insert an image
- position an image
- resize an image
- move footer placeholders (frames)
- switch to Normal view to check the positioning of items
- format the background colour
- insert headers and footers into a master slide:
  - name
  - centre number
  - automatic date
  - automatic date and time
  - slide numbers
- use the different views in PowerPoint
- close a presentation
- exit PowerPoint.

If you think that you need more practice on any of the skills above, go back and work through the skill(s) again.

If you feel confident, move on to Section 2.

## 2: Enter data on slides and print slides

### LEARNING OUTCOMES

**In this section you will learn how to:**

- open a saved presentation
- go to Normal view
- insert new slides
- select an appropriate slide layout
- delete the title slide
- enter text on slides
- promote and demote text
- check the spelling
- use the different print options in PowerPoint
- print all slides and selected slides as individual slides
- print all slides and selected slides as handouts
- insert headers and footers for an Outline view print
- print all slides and selected slides as an Outline view.

## Opening a saved presentation

**▶▶ How to...** open a saved presentation

If it is not already open, start PowerPoint.

1. Click on the **File** menu.
2. Click on **Open**.
3. The **Open** dialogue box is displayed (Figure 5.24).
4. Click on the drop-down arrow next to **Look in**.
5. Go to the user area (folder) where your presentation is saved.
6. Click on the name of the presentation to be opened.
7. Click on **Open**.
8. The presentation will open. If the presentation opens in Slide Master view, click on the **View** menu and click on **Normal**.

**TIP!**

Alternatively, click the Open icon on the Standard toolbar to go to step 4 quickly.

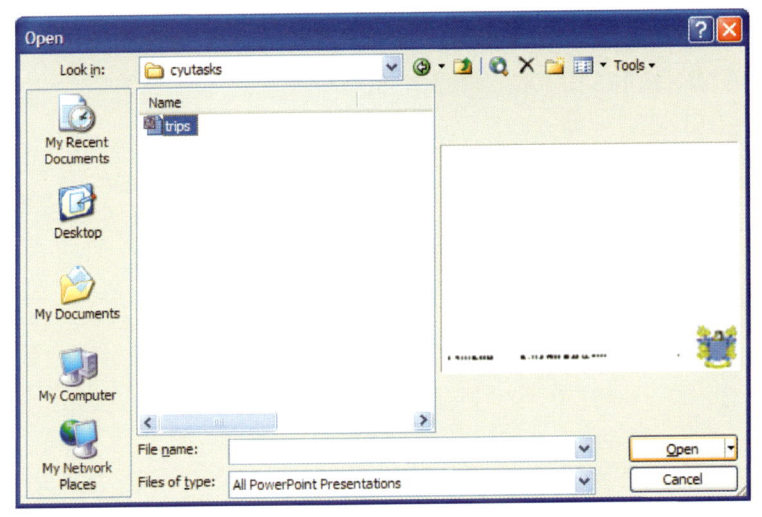

**FIGURE 5.24** The Open dialogue box

## Check your understanding  Open a saved presentation

Open your saved presentation **trips**. Check that you are in Normal view.

## Inserting a new slide

### ▶▶ How to... insert a new slide

1 Click on the **New Slide** button [New Slide] on the **Formatting** toolbar.

2 The **Slide layout** task pane will display on the right of the screen (Figure 5.25) and a new slide will be displayed in the centre of the screen.

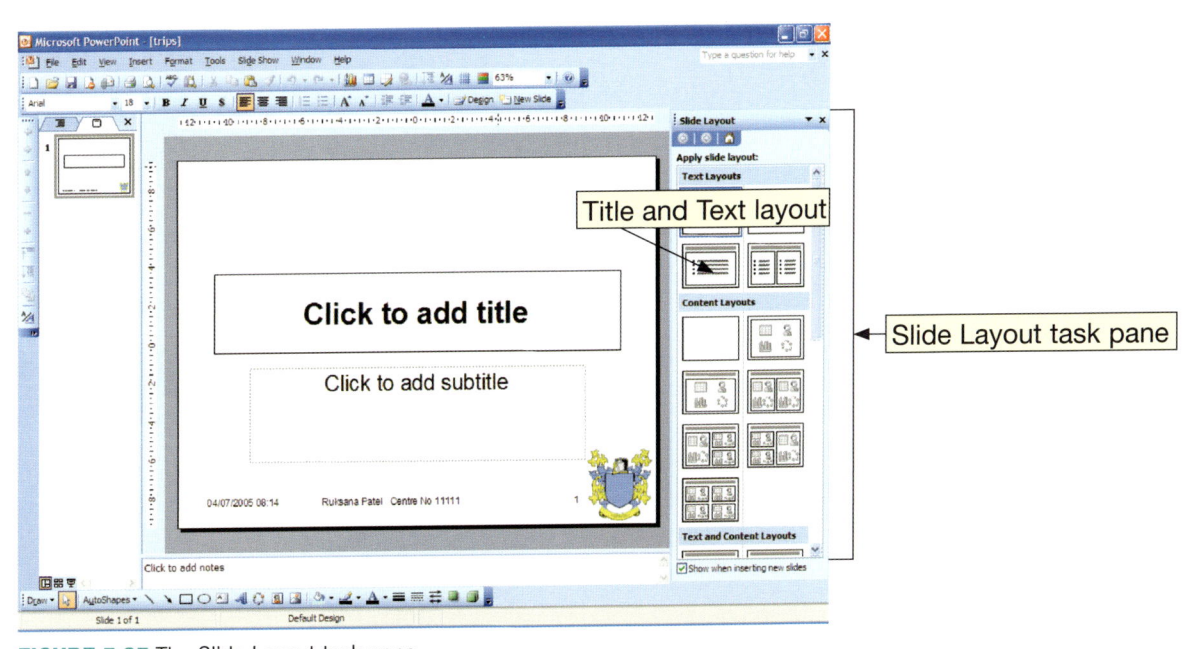

**FIGURE 5.25** The Slide Layout task pane

Section 2: Enter data on slides and print slides    29

3  Look at the **Apply slide layout** section in the task pane.

4  In the **Text Layouts** section, there are miniatures of four different slide layouts.

5  Hover your mouse on each of these layouts.

6  The layout you should always use is the **Title and Text** layout (Figure 5.25).

7  Click on the **Title and Text** layout.

8  This layout should now be displayed in the centre of your screen (Figure 5.26).

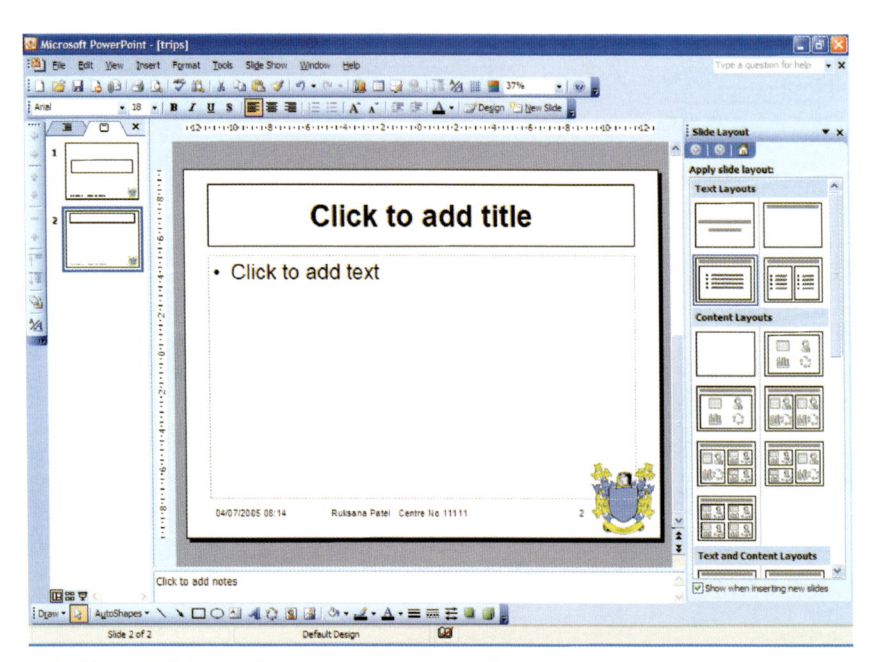

**FIGURE 5.26** Title and Text layout displayed in the centre of the screen

## Check your understanding  *Insert a new slide*

1  In your presentation **trips**, insert a new slide.

2  Select the **Title and Text** layout.

Unit 5: Create an e-presentation

# Understanding the importance of a consistent slide layout

PowerPoint 2003 displays a title slide as the first slide. You must, however, delete this title slide. If you enter text on the title slide you will have an inconsistent slide layout. If you do not delete the title slide, you will also have a blank slide as the first slide.

### ▶▶ How to... delete the title slide

1 In the **Slides** pane on the left of the screen.
2 Click on **slide 1** (the title slide) (Figure 5.27).
3 Press the **Delete** key.

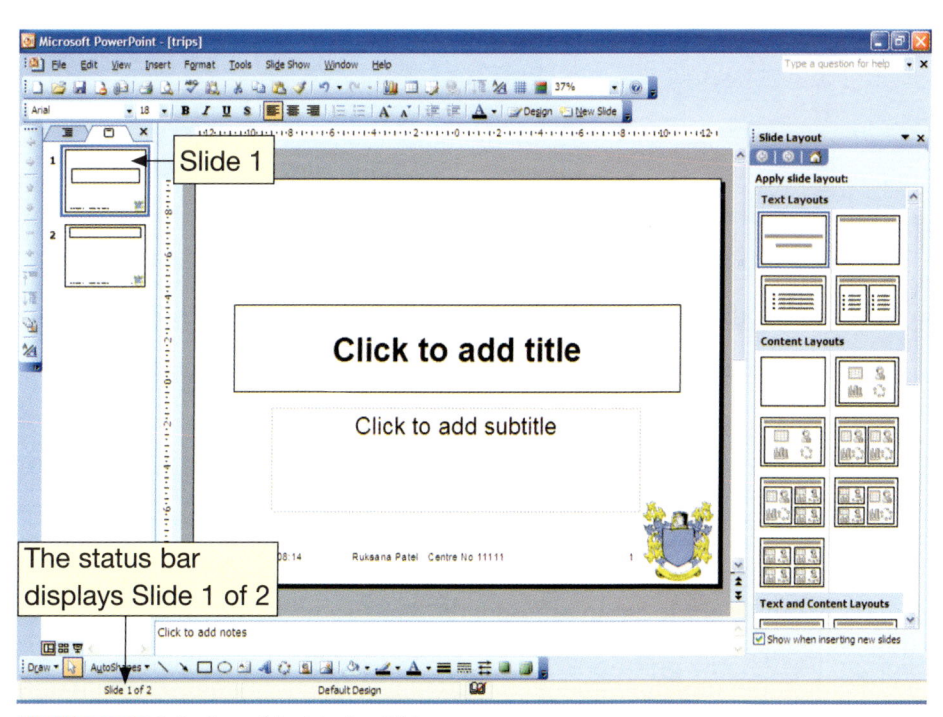

FIGURE 5.27 Selecting slide 1 in the Slides pane

4 Look at the Status bar at the bottom left of your screen. This should now display **Slide 1 of 1**.

### Check your understanding  Delete the title slide

1 In your **presentation trips**, delete slide 1 (the title slide).
2 Save your presentation keeping the filename **trips**.

Section 2: Enter data on slides and print slides

# Entering text on a slide

Make sure you are in Normal view.

**▶▶ How to...** **enter text on a slide**

1. In the title placeholder (frame), click anywhere in the text **Click to add title**.

2. Notice how the text **Click to add title** is deleted automatically and the frame is blank with the cursor flashing in the frame (Figure 5.28).

3. Enter the required title.

4. Do not press the spacebar, the Enter key or the Tab key after you have entered the title.

5. Click in the first line of the main placeholder (frame) in the line **Click to add text**.

6. Notice how the text **Click to add text** is deleted automatically. The cursor is flashing after the bullet character (Figure 5.29).

**FIGURE 5.28** Entering the slide title

7. Enter the required bullet text. The text will be entered as first-level text.

8. Press the **Enter** key to move to the next line if you need to enter text on the next line. Enter the remaining bullet text.

9. If you do not need to enter text on another line, do not press Enter. A bullet character will automatically be displayed on the next line if you press Enter.

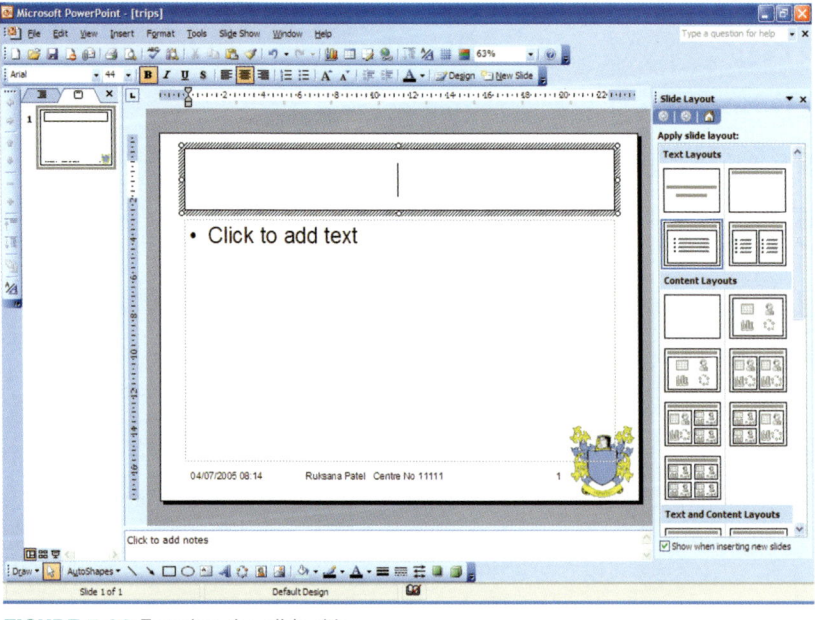

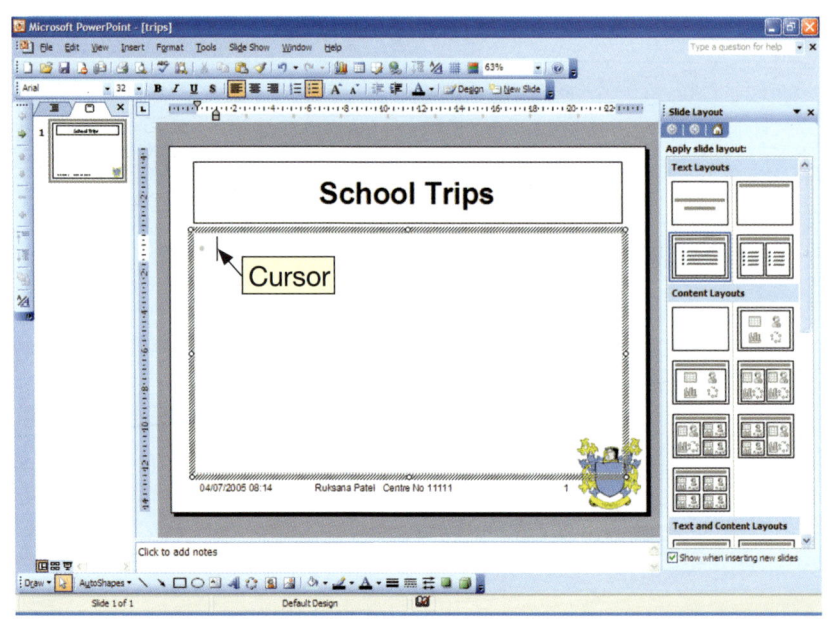

**FIGURE 5.29** Entering first-level text

Unit 5: Create an e-presentation

## Check your understanding — Enter text on slide 1

1 In your presentation **trips**, on slide 1, in the title placeholder enter the title: **School Trips**

2 In the main placeholder enter the following text as first-level text: **Upper Sixth**

3 Save the presentation keeping the filename **trips**.

## Inserting a second new slide

### How to... insert a second new slide

1 Click on the **New Slide** button [New Slide] on the **Formatting** toolbar.
2 A new slide will be displayed in the centre of your screen (Figure 5.30).
3 Check that the **Title and Text** slide layout is displayed.
4 Check that **Slide 2 of 2** is displayed in the Status bar.
5 Check that two slides are displayed in the **Slides** pane on the left of the screen.

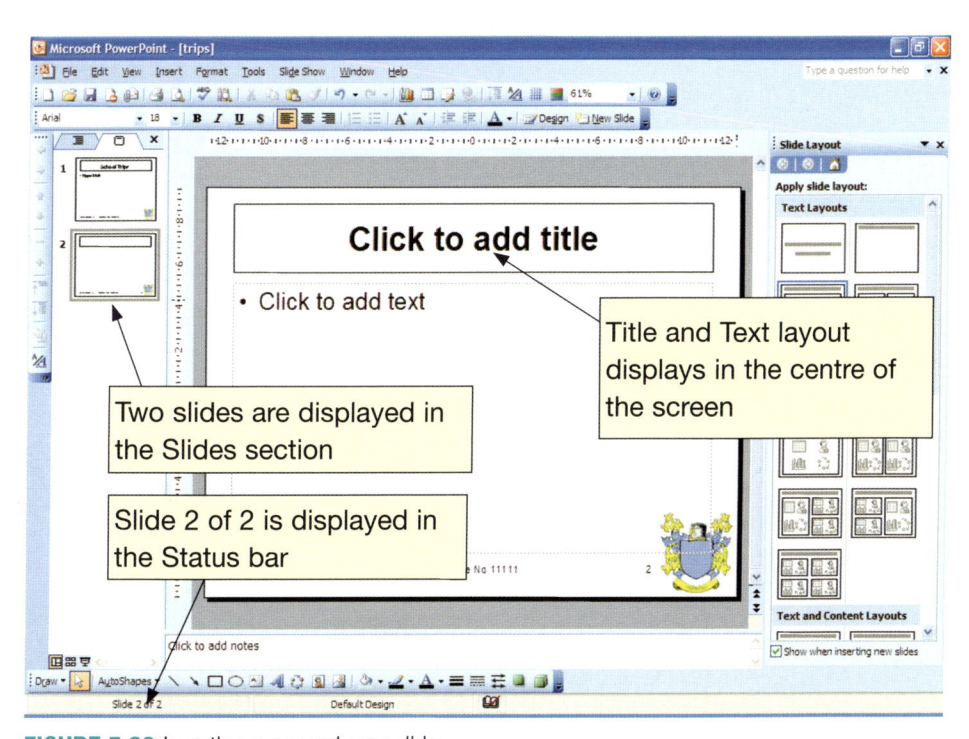

**FIGURE 5.30** Inserting a second new slide

Section 2: Enter data on slides and print slides

### Check your understanding *Insert slide 2*

1 In your presentation **trips**, insert a new slide as slide 2.
2 On slide 2, in the title placeholder, enter the title: **Summer 2007**
3 In the main placeholder enter the following text as first-level bullets:

   **Europe**

   **3 nights Paris**

   **7 days Italy**

   **14 nights Disneyland**

   **Long weekend New York**

4 Save the presentation keeping the filename **trips**.

## Promoting and demoting text

When text is entered in the main placeholder, it is normally displayed as first-level text (i.e. as a main bullet point). However, if the text does not need to stand out as much as the other main bullet points, then it can be moved from being first level to second level. Second-level text is sometimes referred to as sub-bullet text. Second-level text does not stand out as much as first-level text. When you move text from first level to second level, you are said to be *demoting* text.

Similarly, text that is displayed as second level can be moved to become first level. This is referred to as *promoting* text.

There are two ways to promote or demote text:

1 Click on the **Promote** or **Demote** buttons on the **Outlining** toolbar (the Outlining toolbar will need to be displayed).

2 Use the **Decrease Indent** (to promote) or the **Increase Indent** (to demote) icons on the **Formatting** toolbar.

The ▶ *How to...* guidelines that follow refer to the use of the **Increase Indent** and **Decrease Indent** icons as these are easily found on the **Formatting** toolbar. However, you may use the **Promote** and **Demote** icons if you prefer. If so, you will need to display the Outlining toolbar first.

## ▶▶ How to... display the Outlining toolbar

1. Click on the **View** menu.
2. Click on **Toolbars**.
3. If there is no tick in front of **Outlining**, click on **Outlining**.
4. The **Outlining** toolbar will usually be displayed on the left of the screen.

## ▶▶ How to... demote text to become a second-level bullet

1. Click to place your mouse anywhere in the line of text to be demoted.
2. Click on the **Increase Indent** icon on the toolbar (Figure 5.31).
3. The line of text will be demoted to become a sub-bullet.

**TIP!**
If the Outlining toolbar is displayed, you can click on the **Demote** icon instead of **Increase Indent**.

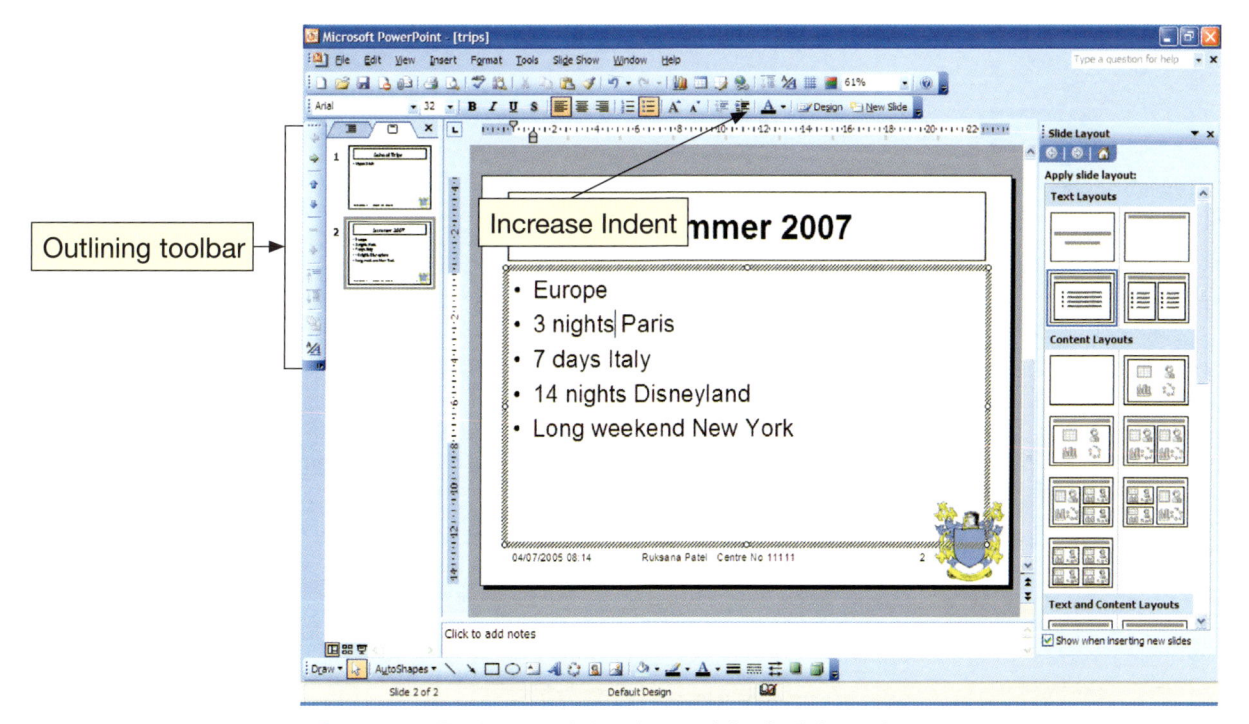

**FIGURE 5.31** The Increase Indent icon and the Outlining toolbar

4. The font type and the style of the bullet character will change.
5. Click in the next line to be demoted and click on the **Increase Indent** icon to demote the next line.
6. Repeat this process for all the other lines that need to be demoted.

**TIP!**
Another method of demoting is to place the cursor at the beginning of the line of text and press the Tab key.

Section 2: Enter data on slides and print slides

## Check your understanding — *Demote text*

1 In your presentation **trips**, on slide 2, demote the following lines of text to become second-level bullets:

   **3 nights Paris**

   **7 days Italy**

   **Long weekend New York**

2 Save your presentation keeping the filename **trips**.

3 Your slide 2 should look similar to Figure 5.32.

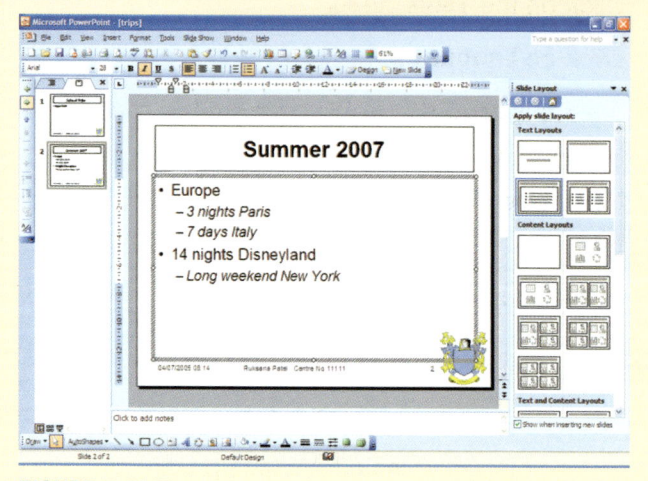

**FIGURE 5.32** The amended slide 2 with text demoted

## Check your understanding — *Insert slide 3*

1 In your presentation **trips**, insert a new slide as slide 3.

2 On slide 3, enter the title: **Winter 2007**

3 Enter the following text and set the styles to first and second-level bullets as shown:

| | |
|---|---|
| **UK** | first-level text |
| **2 days camping** | second-level text |
| **Christmas Lake District** | second-level text |
| **Spain** | first-level text |
| **3 nights city break** | second-level text |
| **7 days Minorca** | second-level text |

4 Save your presentation keeping the filename **trips**.

**TIP!**

If you notice that items overlap after entering text on the slides, go to the Slide Master and make any required changes (e.g. reduce the size of an image, reduce text size, or move the placeholders). All the slides in the presentation will update accordingly.

## Checking the spelling in a presentation

It is very important that you spell check using a UK spell checker. Before you start checking for spelling errors, you must check that the language is set to English UK.

Unit 5: Create an e-presentation

## ▶▶ How to... set the language

1 Click on the **Tools** menu.
2 Click on **Language**.
3 The **Language** dialogue box will be displayed (Figure 5.33).
4 Make sure that the language is set to **English (U.K.)**.
5 Click on **OK**.

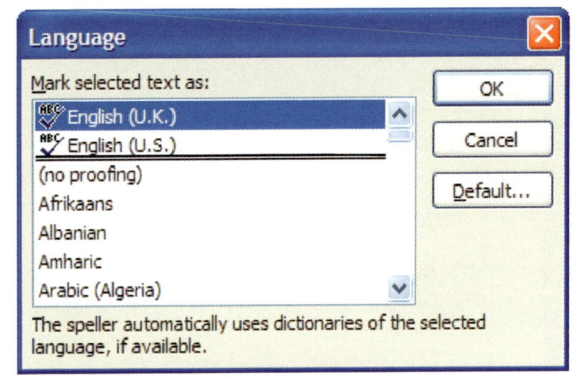

**FIGURE 5.33** The Language dialogue box

## ▶▶ How to... spell check a presentation

1 Click on the **Spelling and Grammar** icon on the Standard toolbar.
2 PowerPoint will check the whole presentation for spelling errors.
3 If an error is found, the **Spelling** dialogue box will be displayed (Figure 5.34).
4 The incorrect word is displayed in the **Not in Dictionary** row.
5 Alternative spellings may be displayed in the **Suggestions** section in the bottom half of the dialogue box.
6 Click on the correct spelling.
7 Click on the **Change** button.
8 PowerPoint will continue to spell check the presentation.
9 When the spell check is complete, a window will be displayed. Click on **OK**.

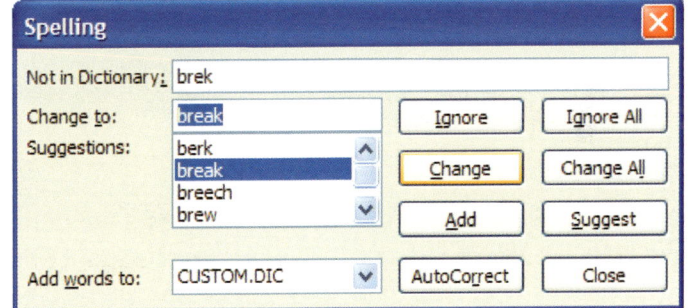

**FIGURE 5.34** The Spelling dialogue box

If the correct spelling is not displayed in the **Suggestions** box:

1 Click on the **Change to** box.
2 Enter the correct spelling.
3 Click on the **Change** button.
4 PowerPoint may display a window asking if you want to make the change.
5 Make sure your spelling is correct, then click on **OK**.

Sometimes PowerPoint will highlight a word as being incorrectly spelt even though it is correct. This is because that word is not in the UK English dictionary (e.g. your name).

Section 2: Enter data on slides and print slides

To ignore a suggested spelling:

1 Make sure that the highlighted word is spelt correctly.

2 Click on the **Ignore Once** button (if you know the word appears only once in the document) or on the **Ignore All** button (if you know the word appears more than once in your presentation).

> ### Check your understanding  *Spell check your presentation*
> 
> 1 In your presentation **trips**, check that the language is set to **English (U.K.)**.
> 
> 2 Spell check your presentation and correct any errors.

## Understanding the print options in PowerPoint

There are many different ways of printing a presentation. Some examples are as follows.

*Individual slides*

- Printing all the slides or selected slides with each slide printed on a separate page.

*Handouts*

- Printing all the slides or selected slides as a set of handouts where the slides are displayed as miniatures. On a handout print, you can choose to display one, two, three, four, six or nine slides on one page. The more slides that are displayed on the page, the smaller the miniature will be.

*Outline view*

- Printing some or all the slides as outlines, which shows only the text on the slides. An Outline view print will not display any headers and footers entered on the master slide or any other objects (e.g. autoshapes, borders, etc.).

Refer to the examples below to help you understand some of the different print options in PowerPoint.

### Print all the slides as individual slides

Every slide in the presentation will be displayed on a separate sheet of paper using the whole page (Figure 5.35).

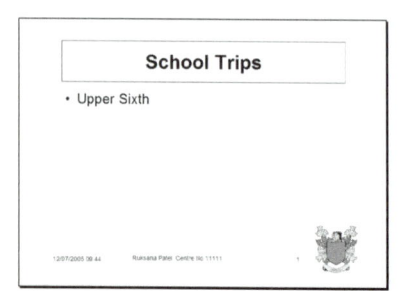

**FIGURE 5.35** Printing all the slides as individual slides

Unit 5: Create an e-presentation

## Print selected slides only

You can choose which of the slide numbers in the presentation you wish to print. Each selected slide will print on a separate sheet of paper.

## Understanding handout prints

A handout print shows an exact replica of a slide as a miniature (smaller). You can choose to display one, two, three, four, six or nine slides as miniatures on one page (Figure 5.36 and 5.37). PowerPoint automatically inserts lines next to the slide miniatures when you print three slides to a page. Handout prints are useful as audience copies of a presentation.

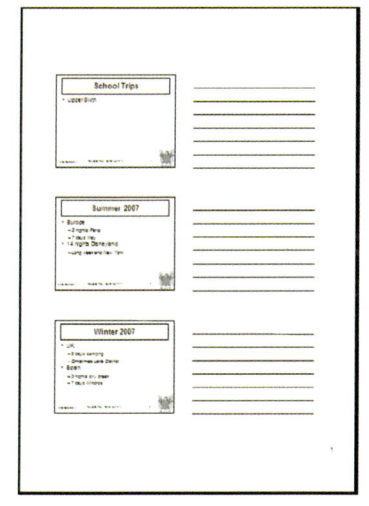

**FIGURE 5.36** Printing three slides to a page

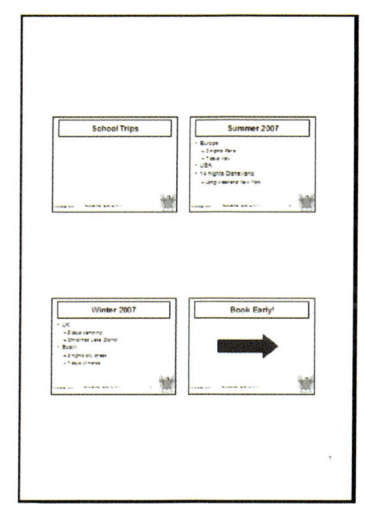

**FIGURE 5.37** Printing four slides to a page

## Understanding Outline view prints

An Outline view print will display only the text on the slides (Figure 5.38). An Outline view printout will not display any:

- headers or footers entered on the master slide
- images on the master slide or on individual slides
- drawing features, graphs, tables, etc.

An Outline view print is useful when you want to check the order and content of the slides in a presentation.

Note: Outline view does not display the headers and footers entered on the master slide.

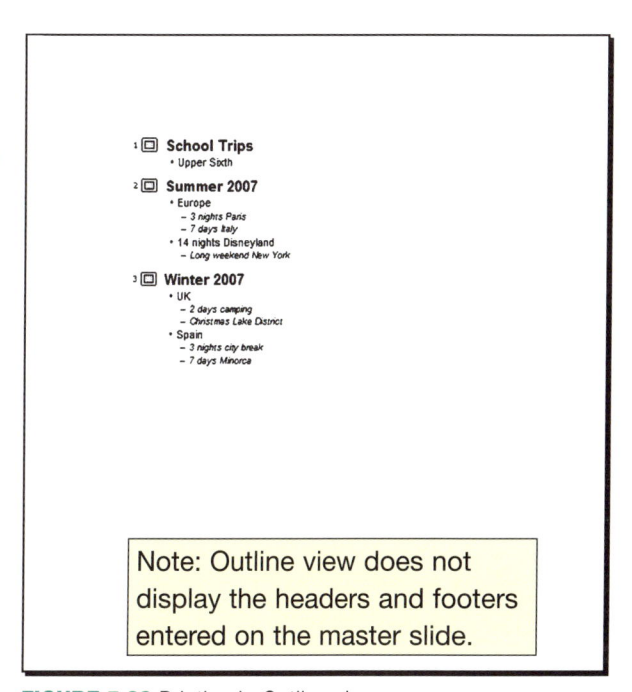

**FIGURE 5.38** Printing in Outline view

Section 2: Enter data on slides and print slides

# Printing slides

**▶▶ How to...** *print all or some slides as individual slides*

1. Click on the **File** menu.
2. Click on **Print**.
3. The **Print** dialogue box will be displayed (Figure 5.39).

To print all the slides:

4. In the **Print range** section, click **All**.
5. Click the **Slides** button and enter the number of each of the slides to be printed, separate each number by a comma (Figure 5.40).

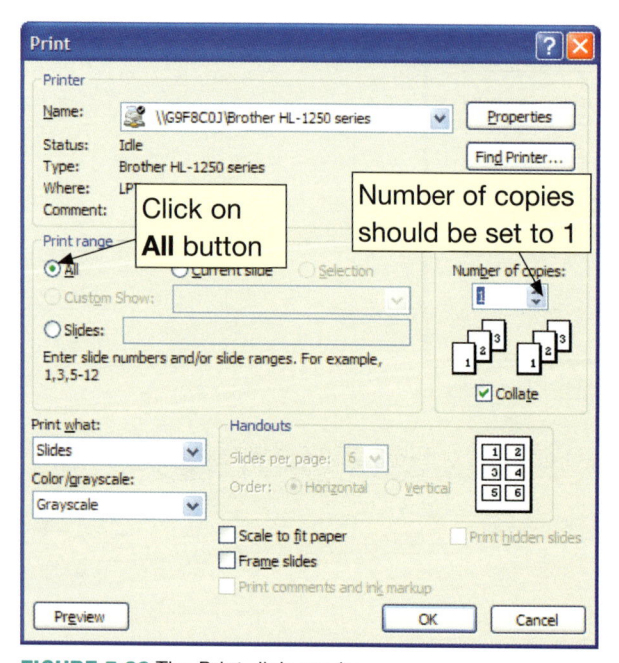

**FIGURE 5.39** The Print dialogue box

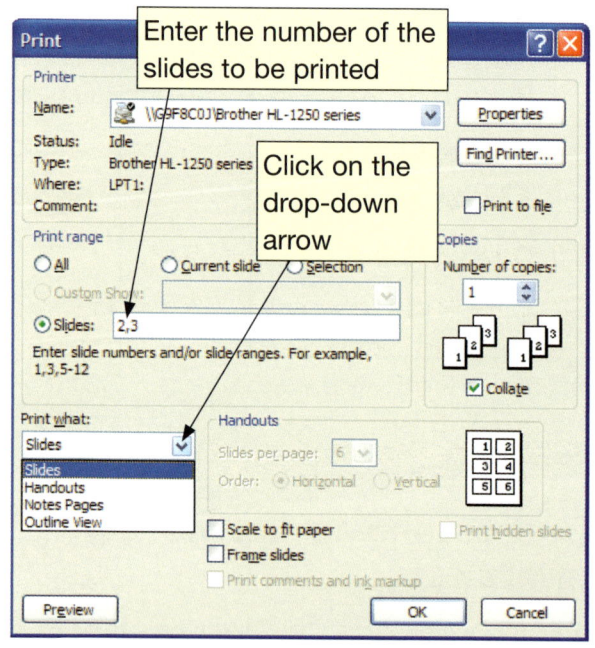

**FIGURE 5.40** Selecting the type of printout and the slide numbers

To print some slides only:

6. Click on the drop-down arrow below **Print what**.
7. A list will be displayed.
8. Click on **Slides**. Enter the number of each of the slides to be printed, separate each number by a comma (Figure 5.40).
9. Check that the **Number of copies** is set to **1**.
10. Click on **OK**.

40   *Unit 5: Create an e-presentation*

## Check your understanding — Print the presentation as slides

1 In your presentation **trips**, print out all three slides, one per page.

2 Each slide should be printed on a separate page.

3 Print only slide 2 as an individual slide.

### ▶▶ How to... print all or some slides in a presentation as handouts

1 Click on the **File** menu.

2 Click on **Print**.

3 The **Print** dialogue box will be displayed.

4 In the **Print range** section, click on the **All** button, OR to print some slides only click on the **Slides** button and enter the number of each of the slides to be printed, separate each number by a comma (Figure 5.42).

5 Click on the drop-down arrow below **Print what**.

6 A list will be displayed.

7 Click on **Handouts** (Figure 5.41).

8 In the **Handouts** section, click on the drop-down arrow next to **Slides per page** (Figure 5.42).

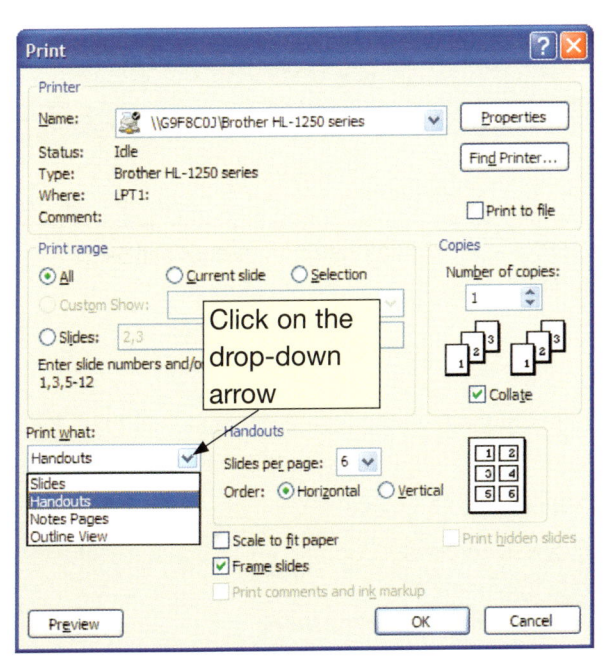

FIGURE 5.41 Selecting Handouts

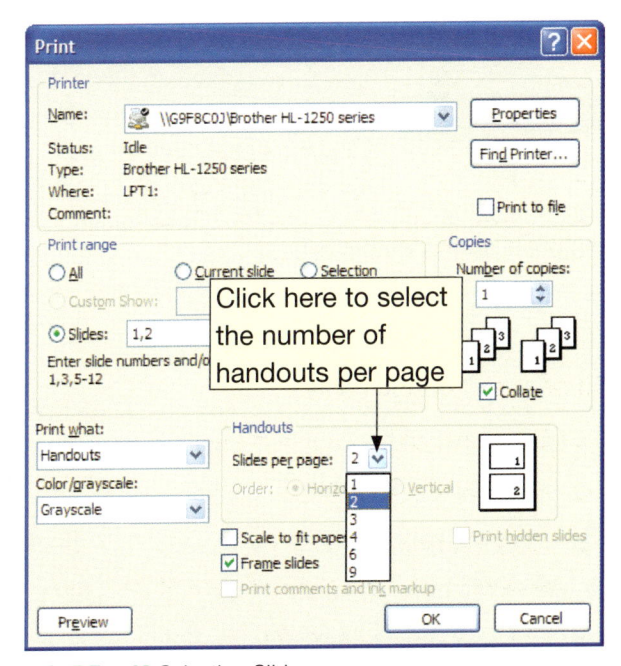

FIGURE 5.42 Selecting Slides per page

Section 2: Enter data on slides and print slides   41

9  Click on the number of slides required on each page.

10  The layout of the handout print will be displayed in the preview on the right.

11  Click on **OK**.

> **Check your understanding**  *Print the presentation as handouts*
>
> 1  In your presentation **trips**, print out all the slides as handouts, three per page.
>
> 2  Print slides 1 and 2 as handouts, two per page.

### ▶▶ How to... insert headers and footers for an Outline view printout

1  Click on the **View** menu.

2  Click on **Header and Footer**.

3  The **Header and Footer** dialogue box will be displayed (Figure 5.43).

4  Click on the tab for **Notes and Handouts**.

5  Click in the box for **Header** or in the box for **Footer**.

6  Enter the required text (e.g. name and centre number).

7  Click on **Apply to All**.

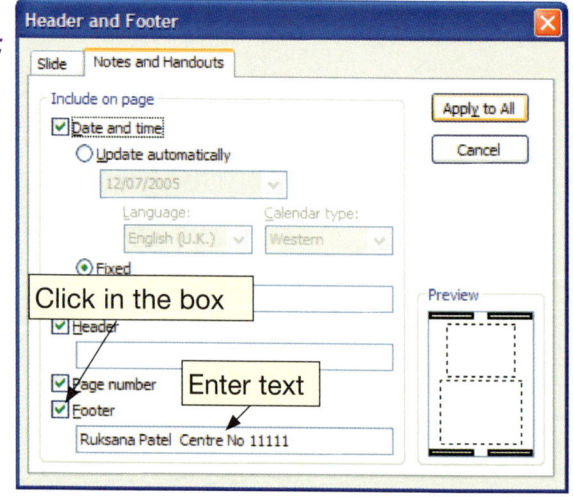

FIGURE 5.43 The Header and Footer dialogue box

### ▶▶ How to... print all or some slides in a presentation as an Outline view

1  Click on the **File** menu.

2  Click on **Print**.

3  The **Print** dialogue box will be displayed.

4  In the **Print range** section, click on the **All** button, OR click the **Slides** button and enter the slide numbers, separated by commas.

5  Click on the drop-down arrow below **Print what**.

6  A list will be displayed.

7  Click on **Outline View** (Figure 5.44).

8  Check that the **Number of copies** is set to **1**.

9  Click on **OK**.

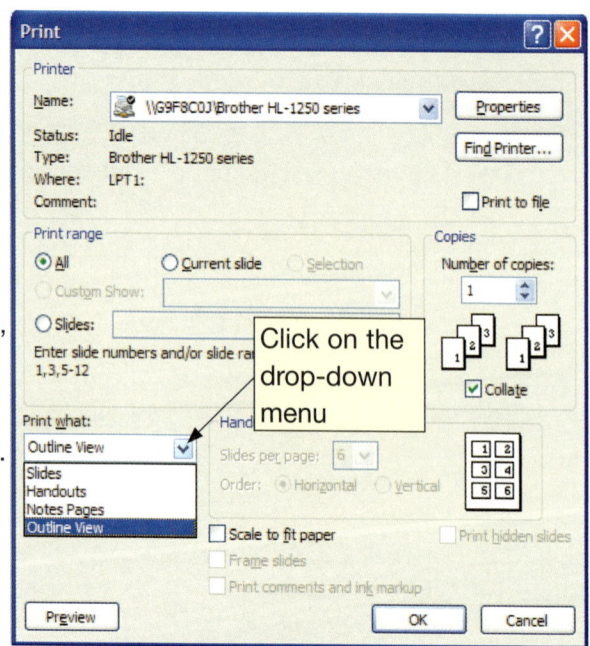

FIGURE 5.44 Selecting Outline view

Unit 5: Create an e-presentation

## Check your understanding
### Print the presentation as an Outline view and exit PowerPoint

1 In your presentation **trips**, enter your name and centre number as a header or footer for Notes and Handouts.
2 Print out **all** the slides as an Outline view print.
3 Save your presentation keeping the filename **trips**.
4 Close the presentation **trips**.
5 Exit PowerPoint.

**TIP!**
Check that the headers and footers are displayed on the printout.

## ASSESS YOUR SKILLS – Enter data on slides and print slides

By working through Section 2 you will have learnt the skills below. Read each item to help you decide how confident you feel about each skill.

- open a saved presentation
- go to Normal view
- insert new slides
- select an appropriate slide layout
- delete the title slide
- enter text on slides
- promote and demote text
- check the spelling
- use the different print options in PowerPoint
- print all slides and selected slides as individual slides
- print all slides and selected slides as handouts
- insert headers and footers for an Outline view print
- print all slides and selected slides as an Outline view.

If you think that you need more practice on any of the skills above, go back and work through the skill(s) again.

If you feel confident, move on to Section 3.

# 3: Update a presentation

## LEARNING OUTCOMES

**In this section you will learn how to:**

- delete text
- save a presentation with a new filename
- delete a placeholder
- insert text
- save an existing presentation
- insert a new slide into an existing presentation
- insert a drawn graphic (e.g. shapes, arrows)
- fill the drawn graphic
- promote and demote text
- find and replace text
- change the order of slides
- run a presentation.

## Deleting text and saving a presentation with a new filename

### ▶▶ How to... delete text

1 Click at the end of the line of text to be deleted.

2 Press the **Backspace** key to delete the line of text and the bullet character. Make sure that the bullet character is also deleted.

3 If there is no other text in the main placeholder, **Click to add text** will be displayed. Don't worry, this text will not print and you will learn how to delete a placeholder.

### ▶▶ How to... save a presentation with a new filename

1 Click on the **File** menu.

2 Click on **Save As**.

3 The **Save As** dialogue box is displayed.

4 Click on the down arrow next to the **Save in** box and double-click to open your working folder.

> **TIP!**
>
> Use the **Delete** key to delete text to the right of the cursor. Use the **Backspace** key to delete text to the left of the cursor.

Unit 5: Create an e-presentation

5 In the **File name** row, delete the existing filename.

6 Enter the new filename.

7 Click on the **Save** button.

8 The presentation will be saved with the new filename in your folder.

### Check your understanding  *Delete text*

1 If it is not already open, start PowerPoint.

2 Open your saved presentation **trips**.

3 On slide 1, delete the text: **Upper Sixth**

4 Make sure that you delete the bullet character.

5 Save your presentation using the new filename **trips2** into the folder you created earlier called **cyu tasks**.

**TIP!**

If you accidentally delete text, click on the **Undo** icon on the Standard toolbar.

## Deleting a placeholder

To delete a placeholder, you must first select the placeholder correctly.

### ▶▶ How to... *select a placeholder*

1 Click on the actual border of the placeholder.

2 The outline of the border will change slightly. In Figure 5.45, the border *has* been selected, but the border in Figure 5.46 *has not* been selected. Notice how the border styles are different.

3 When the main placeholder on a slide is selected, the text **Click to add text** will be displayed in the placeholder.

The placeholder is selected. The cursor will not flash in the main placeholder and **Click to add text** will be displayed

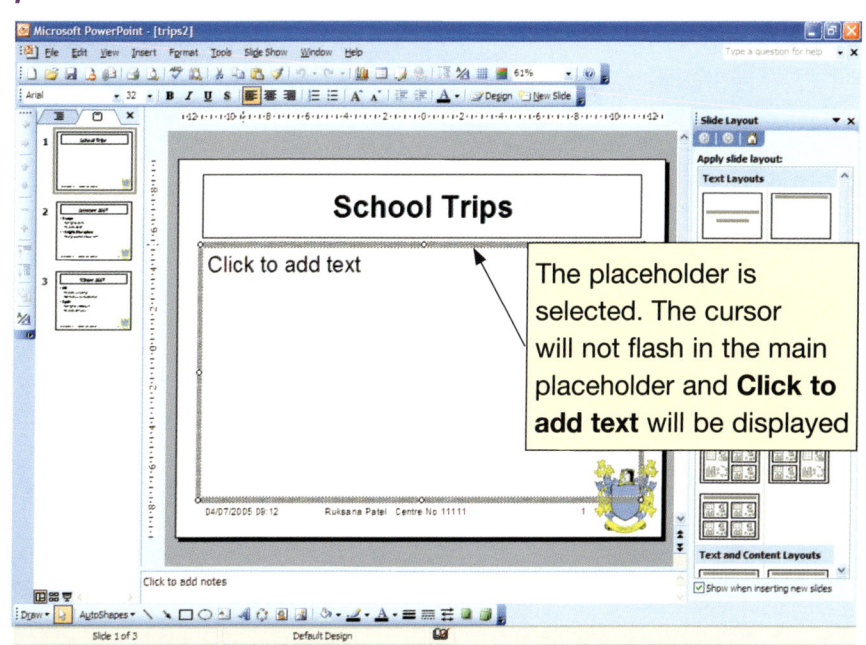

**FIGURE 5.45** Border is selected

Section 3: Update a presentation

### ▶▶ How to... delete a placeholder

1. With the placeholder selected, press the **Delete** key on the keyboard.
2. The placeholder will be deleted.

*The placeholder is not selected. The cursor will flash on the screen in the main placeholder*

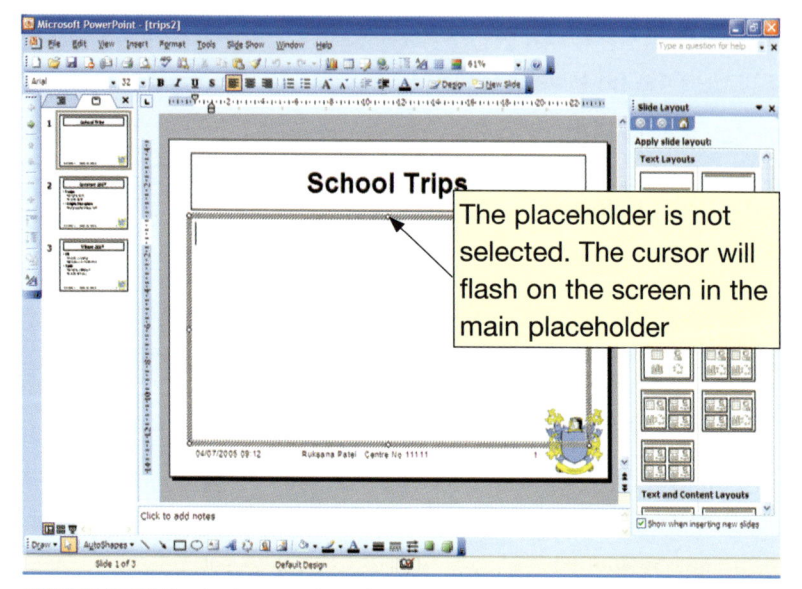

**FIGURE 5.46** Border is not selected

### Check your understanding  Delete the main placeholder

1. In your presentation **trips2**, on slide 1 delete the main placeholder.
2. Save the presentation keeping the filename **trips2**.

## Inserting text into an existing slide and saving an existing presentation

### ▶▶ How to... insert text in the main placeholder on an existing slide

1. Click to place the cursor at the end of the previous line of text.
2. Press the **Enter** key.
3. If required, click on the **Increase Indent** or **Decrease Indent** icon on the **Formatting** toolbar so that the text will be entered correctly as first-level or second-level.
4. Enter the required text.
5. Make sure the text has been entered at the correct level.

### Check your understanding  Insert text into an existing slide

1. In your presentation **trips2**, on slide 2 entitled **Summer 2007**, add the following line of text after **7 days Italy**:

   USA           first-level bullet

2. Save your presentation keeping the filename **trips2**.

Unit 5: Create an e-presentation

# Inserting a new slide into an existing presentation

When you click the **New Slide** button on the Formatting toolbar, a new slide will be inserted after the slide currently displayed on the screen. Therefore, before you click the **New Slide** button, you must make sure that you check which slide is currently selected.

## ▶▶ How to... check which slide is currently selected

1. Check the Status bar at the bottom left of the screen to see which slide is the current slide.
2. The current slide will display as well as the total number of slides in the presentation.
3. In the **Slides** section on the left of the screen, a darker border (usually blue) will be displayed around the current slide.

**TIP!**
If you insert a new slide in the wrong position, refer to How to... change the order of slides on page 51.

## ▶▶ How to... move between slides

1. Find the **Page Up** and **Page Down** keys on your keyboard.
2. Click on the **Page Up** key to move to previous slides, or click on the **Page Down** key to move to subsequent slides.
3. Check the Status bar and the **Slides** section to see that the slide selected is the one *before* the position in which you want to insert a new slide.
4. Click on the **New Slide** button.
5. Check to make sure that the **Title and Text** layout is selected.

**TIP!**
The **Page Down** key may be marked as **Page Dn**, **PgDn** or **Pg Down**. The **Page Up** key may be marked as **Page Up**, **PgUp** or **Pg Up**.

### Check your understanding
*Insert a new slide into an existing presentation*

1. In your presentation **trips2**, insert a new slide as slide 4.
2. On slide 4, enter the title:

   **Book Early!**
3. Save your presentation keeping the filename **trips2**.

# Drawing a graphic shape

Before you begin, check that the Drawing toolbar is displayed.

## ▶▶ How to... draw a shape in the main slide area

1. Delete the main placeholder.
2. On the Drawing toolbar, click on **AutoShapes**.

Section 3: Update a presentation

3 A list of shapes will be displayed (Figure 5.47).

4 Click on the category of the shape required (e.g. Basic Shapes, Block Arrows or Callouts).

5 A selection of shapes will display (Figure 5.47).

6 Click on the required shape.

7 The mouse turns to a + (cross).

8 Move your mouse into the main placeholder area.

9 Click and drag the mouse to draw the shape.

10 The shape may be filled with a colour automatically, ignore the colour for the moment as you will learn how to change the fill colour.

**TIP!**

Avoid clicking in the placeholder once you have selected the required shape – you should click and drag. If you click once with the mouse, the size of the shape will be created automatically, however, by clicking and dragging, you can draw a shape to an exact size.

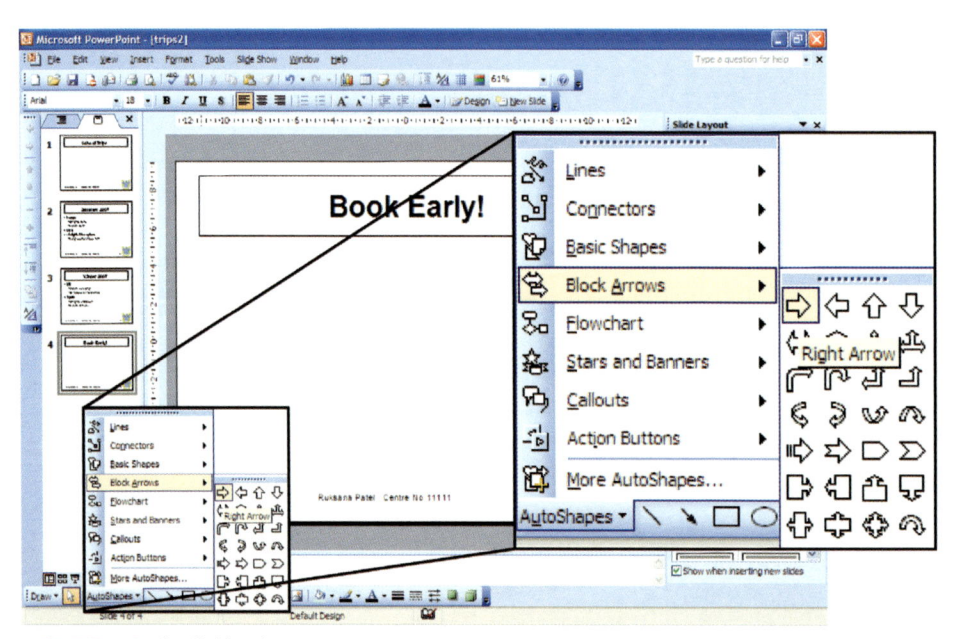

**FIGURE 5.47** Available shapes

**TIP!**

To move or resize a shape, refer to How to… position an image and How to… resize an image on pages 19 and 20.

## Check your understanding  *Draw a shape*

1 In your presentation **trips2**, on slide 4, entitled **Book Early!**, in the main slide area below the title placeholder, create an arrow pointing to the right as shown in Figure 5.48.

2 Make sure that you draw the arrow between the title and the footer area, in the main slide area.

3 Make sure that the arrow does not touch or overlap the image at the right-hand corner of the slide or the title or the footer text.

4 Save your presentation keeping the filename **trips2**.

**FIGURE 5.48** Drawing a shape

48  Unit 5: Create an e-presentation

# Filling a graphic with a colour

### ▶▶ How to... fill a graphic with a colour

1 Make sure the graphic is selected – round handles should be displayed around it.

2 If there are no handles visible around the graphic, click on it once and handles should be displayed indicating that it is selected.

3 On the Drawing toolbar, click on the drop-down arrow next to the **Fill Color** icon.

4 A window will open displaying various colours (Figure 5.49).

5 Click on one of the colour squares.

6 The shape will be filled with the colour chosen.

> **TIP!**
> Use a dark colour as this will display more clearly on a printout.

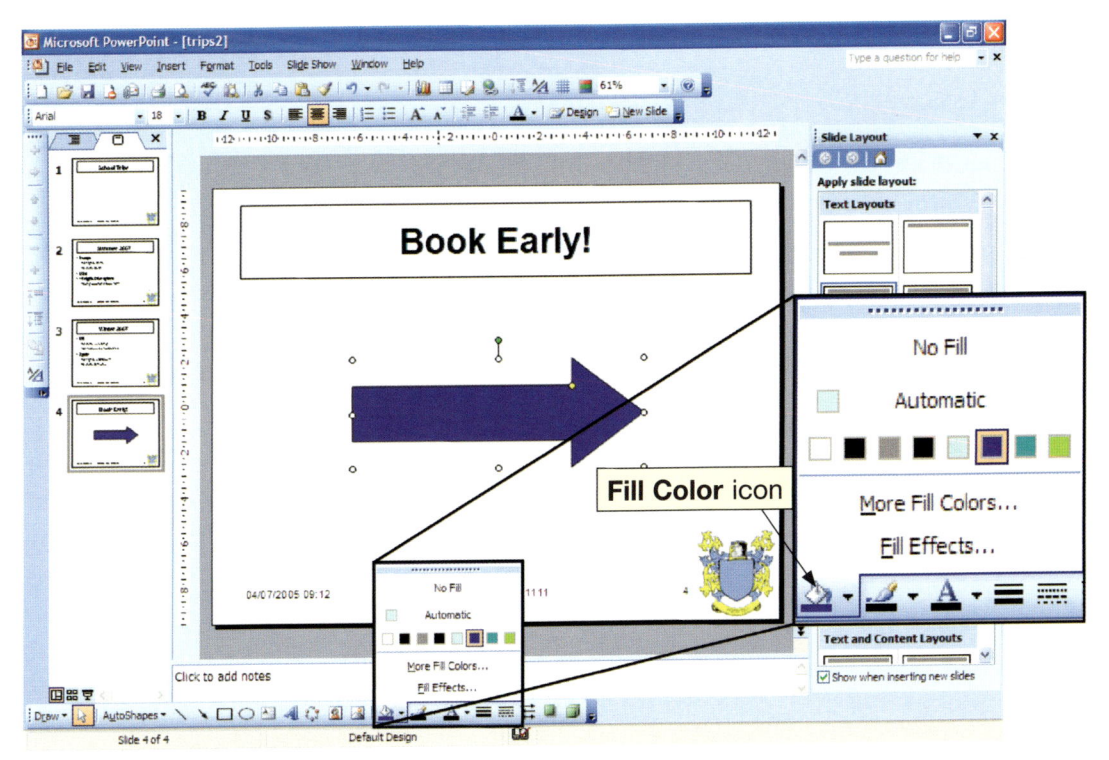

**FIGURE 5.49** Colours available

### Check your understanding  Fill a drawn graphic with a colour

1 In your presentation **trips2**, on slide 4, entitled **Book Early!**, fill the arrow with a dark colour.

2 Save your presentation keeping the filename **trips2**.

3 Print the presentation as an Outline view to display the text on all four slides.

4 Make sure that your name and centre number are displayed on the printout.

Section 3: Update a presentation    49

## Promoting and demoting text

**▶▶ How to...** promote second-level text to become first-level text on an existing slide

1 Click anywhere in the line of text to be promoted.
2 On the **Formatting** toolbar, click on the **Increase Indent** icon.
3 The line of text will be promoted to become first-level text.

**TIP!**
Alternatively, use the Promote or Demote icon on the Outlining toolbar.

**▶▶ How to...** demote first-level text to become second-level text on an existing slide

1 Click anywhere in the line of text to be demoted.
2 On the **Formatting** toolbar, click on the **Decrease Indent** icon.
3 The line of text will be demoted to become second-level text.

**TIP!**
Alternatively, use the **Tab** key to demote text.

### Check your understanding — Demote text on an existing slide

1 In your presentation **trips2**, on slide 2 titled **Summer 2007**, demote the line **14 nights Disneyland** to become second-level text.
2 Save your presentation using the new filename **trips3**

## Find and replace

**▶▶ How to...** find and replace text

1 Click on the **Edit** menu.
2 Click on **Replace**.
3 The **Replace** dialogue box will be displayed (Figure 5.50).
4 In the **Find what** box enter the word to be replaced.
5 In the **Replace with** box type in the new word.
6 Click to place a tick in the **Match case** box.
7 Click to place a tick in the **Find whole words only** box.
8 Click on **Replace All**.
9 The word will be replaced and PowerPoint will display a window informing you how many replacements were made (Figure 5.51).

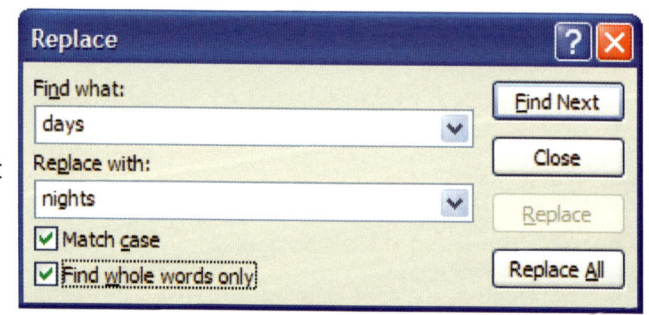

**FIGURE 5.50** The Replace dialogue box

Unit 5: Create an e-presentation

10  Click on **OK**.

11  Click on the **Close** button to close the **Replace** dialogue box.

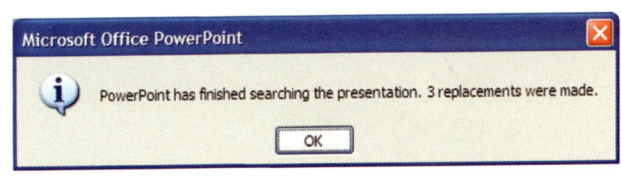

**FIGURE 5.51** The number of replacements made

> ### Check your understanding  *Replace text*
>
> 1  In your presentation **trips3**, replace the word **days** with the word **nights** wherever it appears in the presentation (three times in all).
>
> 2  Make sure you match the case and that you find whole words only.
>
> 3  Save your presentation keeping the filename **trips3**.

## Changing the order of the slides

▶▶ **How to...**  *change the order of the slides*

The slide order can be changed from the **Slides** pane on the left of the screen or in **Slide Sorter** view.

1  In the Slides pane or in Slide Sorter view, click once on the slide to be moved.

2  Check that the slide is selected (the border will become a darker shade).

3  Click on the **Edit** menu.

4  Click on **Cut**.

5  The slide will no longer be displayed on screen.

6  Click with the mouse in the position *after* the slide where you want to move the slide to.

7  A flashing line will be displayed to indicate the position.

8  Click on the **Edit** menu.

9  Click on **Paste**.

10  The slide will be moved to the new position.

Another method of changing the order of slides is to click on the slide to be moved and to drag it to the required position.

## Check your understanding
### Insert and resize an image and change the slide order

Refer to Section 1 for How to… insert, position and resize an image.

1. In your presentation **trips3**, on slide 1 titled **School Trips**, insert the image **six** below the heading and above the footer text.
2. Resize the image **six** so that it is larger than it was originally.
3. Make sure that you do not distort the image.
4. Change the order of the slides so that slide 4 entitled **Book Early!** becomes slide 2.
5. Save your presentation keeping the filename **trips3**.
6. Print the presentation as handouts with four slides on one page.
7. Close the presentation.

## How to... run a presentation

1. Check that the current view is Normal (Figure 5.52).
2. Check the Status bar to make sure **slide 1** is selected. If not, press the **Page Up** key on your keyboard to go to slide 1.
3. Locate the icon for **Slide Show from current slide** (above the Drawing toolbar).
4. Click this icon. Slide 1 will be displayed on the full screen with no menus, toolbars, etc.

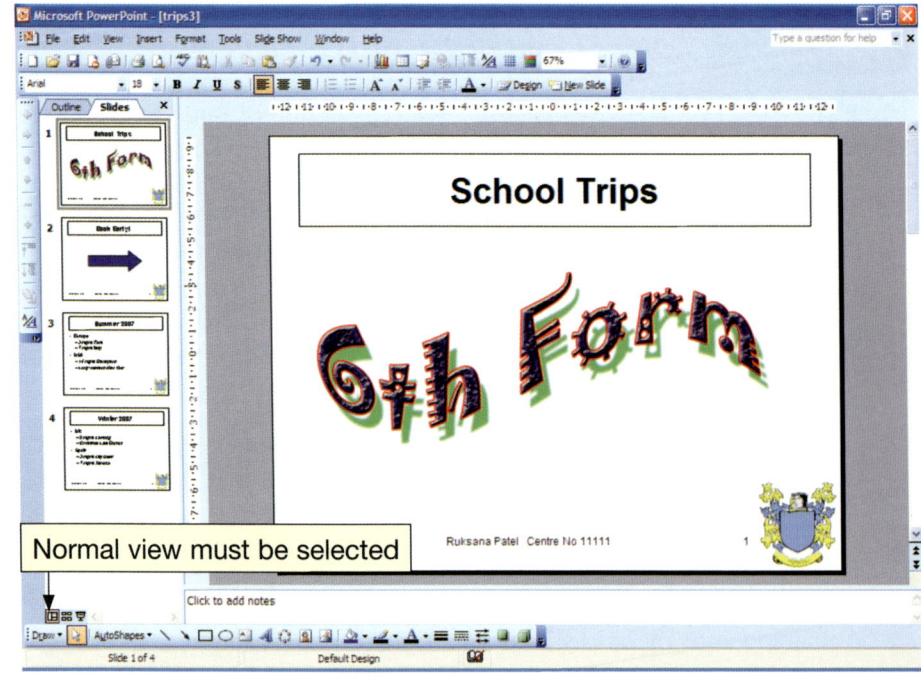

**FIGURE 5.52** Normal view

5. Click on the **Page Down** key on your keyboard to move to the next slide.
6. When you run the last slide, a blank screen will be displayed with **End of slide show**, **click to exit** at the top of the screen.
7. Click once to return to Normal view.

Unit 5: Create an e-presentation

## Check your understanding — *Run your presentation*

1. Run your presentation by clicking the icon for **Slide Show from current slide**.
2. When you have viewed all four slides, return to Normal view.
3. Save your presentation, and exit PowerPoint.

## ASSESS YOUR SKILLS – Update a presentation

By working through Section 3 you will have learnt the skills below. Read each item to help you decide how confident you feel about each skill.

- delete text
- save a presentation with a new filename
- delete a placeholder
- insert text
- save an existing presentation
- insert a new slide into an existing presentation
- insert a drawn graphic (e.g. shapes, arrows)
- fill the drawn graphic
- promote text
- demote text
- find and replace text
- insert an image into a slide
- resize an image
- change the order of slides
- run a presentation.

If you think that you need more practice on any of the skills above, go back and work through the skill(s) again.

If you feel confident, do the Build-up and Practice tasks that start on page 61.

Remember, you can refer to the **Quick reference guides** starting on page 54 when doing any tasks and during an assessment.

# QUICK REFERENCE – Create a master slide

**Click** means click with the left mouse button

Keep a copy of this page next to you. Refer to it when working through tasks and during any assessments.

| HOW TO... | METHOD |
|---|---|
| Start PowerPoint | Click the Start button → All Programs → Microsoft Office → Microsoft Office PowerPoint 2003. |
| Create a new presentation | Click the File menu → New. *Note:* A new blank presentation opens when you load PowerPoint. |
| Go to Slide Master view | Click the View menu → Master → Slide Master. |
| Set the slide orientation | Click the File menu → Page Setup → in the Slides section, click on Portrait or Landscape → OK. |
| Set the text emphasis (enhancement) for the title | Click in the text Click to edit Master title style → the text will be highlighted → on the Formatting toolbar, click on the icon(s) for the required emphasis (bold, italic or underline). |
| Set the text size for the title | Click in the text Click to edit Master title style → the text will be highlighted → on the Formatting toolbar, click the drop-down arrow to the right of the Font Size box → from the drop-down list, click on the required size. |
| Set the text alignment for the title | Click in the text Click to edit Master title style → the text will be highlighted → on the Formatting toolbar, click on the icon for the required alignment (left, centre or right). |
| Set the text emphasis (enhancement) for the first-level text | Click in the text Click to edit Master text style → the text will be highlighted → on the Formatting toolbar, click on the icon(s) for the required emphasis (bold, italic or underline). |
| Set the text size for the first-level text | Click in the text Click to edit Master text style → the text will be highlighted → on the Formatting toolbar, click the drop-down arrow to the right of the Font Size box → from the drop-down list, click on the required size. |
| Set the text alignment for the first-level text | Click in the text Click to edit Master text style → the text will be highlighted → on the Formatting toolbar, click on the icon for the required alignment (left, centre or right). |
| Set the text emphasis (enhancement) for the second-level text | Click in the text Second level → the text will be highlighted → on the Formatting toolbar, click on the icon(s) for the required emphasis (bold, italic or underline). |

Unit 5: Create an e-presentation

| HOW TO… | METHOD |
|---|---|
| Set the text size for the second-level text | Click in the text Second level → the text will be highlighted → on the Formatting toolbar, click the drop-down arrow to the right of the Font Size box → from the drop-down list, click on the required size. |
| Set the text alignment for the second-level text | Click in the text Second level → the text will be highlighted → on the Formatting toolbar, click on the icon for the required alignment (left, centre or right). |
| Display the Drawing toolbar | Click the View menu → Toolbars. If there is no tick in front of Drawing, click Drawing. |
| Create a border | Click in the placeholder or click on the image for which you want to create a border → on the Drawing toolbar, click on the Line Style or the Dash Style icon → a selection of available styles displays → click on a suitable style. |
| Set the border colour | Click to select the placeholder or image for which you have created a border → on the Drawing toolbar, click the drop-down arrow next to the Line Color icon → a window will open displaying various colours → click on one of the colour squares. |
| Insert an image | Click the Insert menu → Picture → From File → the Insert Picture dialogue box will be displayed → click the drop-down arrow next to the Look in box → go to the user area (folder) in which the image is saved → check that All pictures is displayed next to the Files of type box → in the main window, click on the name of the image to be inserted → click on Insert. |
| Position an image or a shape | Check to see if round handles are displayed around the image or shape → if not, click on the image or shape once → the handles will be displayed → position the mouse anywhere in the image or shape → the mouse pointer will change to a four-headed arrow → click and drag the image or shape to the required position. |
| Resize an image or a shape | Position the mouse on a corner handle of the image or shape → the mouse will turn into a diagonal double-headed arrow → to reduce the image or shape size: click and drag the double-headed arrow inwards → to increase the image or shape size: click and drag the double-headed arrow outwards. |
| Move footer placeholders | Click on the placeholder → hold down the Ctrl key and the cursor key (arrow key) at the same time → tap the cursor key until the placeholder is moved to the required position. |
| Check the positioning of items in Normal view | Click the View menu → Normal. The image and any footer items will be displayed on the slide. |
| Return to Slide Master view | Click the View menu → Master → Slide Master. |
| Format the background colour | Click the Format menu → Background → the Background dialogue box will be displayed → click the drop-down arrow next to the sample colour displayed (usually white) → a selection of colours will be displayed → click on a colour box to select a colour → click on Apply to All. |

(continued overleaf)

Quick reference – Create a master slide   55

| HOW TO... | METHOD |
|---|---|
| Insert name and centre number in a footer on a master slide | Click the View menu → Header and Footer → the Header and Footer dialogue box will be displayed → click to place a tick in the box Footer → enter your name and centre number in the box below Footer. |
| Insert an automatic date | Click the View menu → Header and Footer → the Header and Footer dialogue box will be displayed → click to place a tick in the box Date and time → click in the button Update automatically → click the drop-down arrow next to the date → a list of date and time formats will be displayed → click on an option that displays the date → click on Apply to All. |
| Insert an automatic date and the time | Click the View menu → Header and Footer → the Header and Footer dialogue box will be displayed → click to place a tick in the box Date and time → click in the button Update automatically → click the drop-down arrow next to the date → a list of date and time formats will be displayed → click on an option that displays the date and the time → click on Apply to All. |
| Insert slide numbers | Click the View menu → Header and Footer → the Header and Footer dialogue box will be displayed → click to place a tick in the box Slide number → click on Apply to All. |
| Save a presentation into a new folder | Click the File menu → Save As → the Save As dialogue box will be displayed → click the down arrow to the right of the Save in box → a list of user areas will be displayed → click on your user area → the folder/user area name will be displayed in the Save in box → click on the Create New Folder icon → the New Folder dialogue box will be displayed → type in the new folder name → click on OK → in the File name box, delete any existing text → type in the required filename → make sure Presentation is displayed → click the Save button. |
| Close a presentation | Click the File menu → Close. |
| Exit PowerPoint | Click the File menu → Exit. |

Unit 5: Create an e-presentation

**Click** means click with the left mouse button

## QUICK REFERENCE – Enter data on slides and print slides

Keep a copy of this page next to you. Refer to it when working through tasks and during any assessments.

| HOW TO... | METHOD |
|---|---|
| Open a saved presentation | Click the File menu → Open → click the drop-down arrow next to the Look in box → go to the user area (folder) where your presentation is saved → click on the name of the presentation to be opened → click on Open. |
| Go to Normal view | Click the View menu → Normal. |
| Insert new slides | Click the New Slide button on the Formatting toolbar → a Slide Layout task pane will be displayed on the right of the screen and a new slide will be displayed in the centre of the screen. |
| Select an appropriate slide layout | In the Text Layouts section on the right of the screen, click on the miniature slide image for Title and Text. |
| Enter headings and bulleted text | Click in the title placeholder → click anywhere in the text Click to add title → the text Click to add title will be deleted automatically → enter the required title → click in the main placeholder → the text Click to add text will be deleted automatically → enter the required bullet text → the text will be entered as first-level text → press the Enter key → a bullet character will automatically be displayed on the next line → enter the remaining text. |
| Delete text | Place the cursor after the last character in the line → press the Backspace key to delete the text → make sure the bullet character is also deleted → another method is to highlight the text and the press the Delete key. |
| Save an existing presentation | Click the File menu → Save OR click the Save icon. |
| Print all slides as individual slides | Click the File menu → Print → the Print dialogue box will be displayed → click the All button → click the drop-down arrow below Print what → a list will be displayed → click Slides → check that the Number of copies is set to 1 → click on OK. |
| Print selected slides as individual slides | Click the File menu → Print → the Print dialogue box will be displayed → click the Slides button → in the Slides box, enter the number of each of the slides to be printed, separate each number by a comma → click the drop-down arrow below Print what → a list will be displayed → click Slides → check that the Number of copies is set to 1 → click on OK. |

(continued overleaf)

| HOW TO… | METHOD |
|---|---|
| Print all slides as handouts | Click the File menu → Print → the Print dialogue box will be displayed → click the All button → click the drop-down arrow below Print what → a list will be displayed → click Handouts → in the Handouts section, click the drop-down arrow next to Slides per page → click on the number required → the layout of the handout print will be displayed to the right → check that the Number of copies is set to 1 → click on OK. |
| Print selected slides as handouts | Click the File menu → Print → the Print dialogue box will be displayed → click the Slides button → in the Slides box, enter the number of each of the slides to be printed, separate each number by a comma → click the drop-down arrow below Print what → a list will be displayed → click Handouts → in the Handouts section, click the drop-down arrow next to Slides per page → click on the number required → the layout of the handout print will be displayed to the right → check that the Number of copies is set to 1 → click on OK. |
| Insert headers and footers for an Outline view print | Click the View menu → Header and Footer → the Header and Footer dialogue box will be displayed → click the tab for Notes and Handouts → click in the box for Header or Footer → enter the required text → click on Apply to All. |
| Print all or some slides as an Outline view | Click the File menu → Print → the Print dialogue box will be displayed → click the Slides button → in the Slides box, enter the number of each of the slides to be printed → separate each number by a comma OR click the All button → click the drop-down arrow below Print what → a list will be displayed → click on Outline View → check that the Number of copies is set to 1 → click on OK. |

Unit 5: Create an e-presentation

# QUICK REFERENCE – Update a presentation

*Click means click with the left mouse button*

Keep a copy of this page next to you. Refer to it when working through tasks and during any assessments.

| HOW TO... | METHOD |
|---|---|
| Insert text | Click in the placeholder → enter the text. |
| Insert a new slide into an existing presentation | Click the New Slide button on the Formatting toolbar → the Slide Layout task pane will be displayed on the right of the screen and a new slide will be displayed in the centre → in the Text Layouts section on the right of the screen, click on the miniature for Title and Text. |
| Delete an unwanted placeholder | Click on the border of the placeholder to be deleted → the outline of the border will change and the text Click to add text will be displayed in the placeholder → press the Delete key. |
| Insert a drawn graphic (e.g. shapes, arrows) | Delete the main placeholder → on the Drawing toolbar, click on AutoShapes → a list of shapes will be displayed → click the category of the shape required (e.g. Basic Shapes, Block Arrows or Callouts) → a selection of shapes is displayed → click on the required shape → the mouse will turn to a + (cross) → move the mouse into the main placeholder → click and drag the mouse to draw the shape. |
| Fill the drawn graphic | Make sure the graphic is selected: round handles should be displayed around the graphic → if there are no handles visible around the graphic, click on it once → on the Drawing toolbar, click the drop-down arrow next to the Fill Color icon → a box will open displaying various colours → click on one of the colour squares. |
| Promote text | Click anywhere in the line of text to be promoted → on the Formatting toolbar, click the Decrease Indent icon OR click the Promote icon on the Outlining toolbar. |
| Demote text | Click anywhere in the line of text to be demoted → on the Formatting toolbar, click the Increase Indent icon OR click the Demote icon on the Outlining toolbar OR press the Tab key. |
| Find and replace text | Click the Edit menu → Replace → the Replace dialogue box will be displayed → in the Find what box, enter the word to be replaced → in the Replace with box, type in the new word → click to place a tick in the Match case box → click to place a tick in the Find whole words only box → click on Replace All → a box will be displayed informing you how many replacements were made → click on OK → Close. |

*(continued overleaf)*

Quick reference – Update a presentation 59

| HOW TO... | METHOD |
|---|---|
| Insert an image into a slide | Make sure that the slide on which the image is to be inserted is selected → click the Insert menu → Picture → From File → the Insert Picture dialogue box will be displayed → click the drop-down arrow next to the Look in box → go to the user area (folder) in which the image is saved → check that All pictures is displayed next to the Files of type box → click on the name of the image to be inserted → Insert. |
| Change the order of slides | In the Slides pane on the left of the screen → click once on the slide to be moved → check that the slide is selected (the border will become a darker shade) → click the Edit menu → Cut → the slide will no longer be displayed on screen → click with the mouse in the position *after* the slide where you want to move the slide to → a flashing line will be displayed to indicate the position → click the Edit menu → Paste. |
| Save an existing presentation | Click the File menu → Save (or click the Save icon on the Standard toolbar). |
| Run a presentation | In Normal view, make sure slide 1 is selected → click on the Slide Show from current slide icon → click on the Page Down key to move to the next slide → the blank screen with the message End of slide show, click to exit indicates the last slide has been shown → click once to return to Normal view. |

60  Unit 5: Create an e-presentation

## BUILD-UP TASK 1 *Create a master slide*

You will need the image **mall** from the folder **files_presentations**.

1. Set up a master slide as follows. This master slide layout must be used for all the slides.

   a. Set the slide orientation to **landscape**.

   b. Use the placeholder at the top of the slide for the title.

   c. Use the main placeholder for the slide content.

   d. Set up the text styles as follows:

   | STYLE | EMPHASIS | SIZE | FEATURE | ALIGNMENT |
   |---|---|---|---|---|
   | title | bold only | large | dark border | centre |
   | first-level bullet | italic only | medium | any bullet character | left |
   | second-level bullet | none | small | any bullet character | left and indented from first-level bullet |

   e. Make sure there is at least one character space between the bullets and text.

   f. Place the image **mall** at the bottom right corner of the master slide.

   g. Display a dashed line border around this image.

   h. Make sure the image will not overlap any text. Make sure you maintain the image's original proportions.

   i. In the footer area enter:

   **your name**

   **your centre number**

   **an automatic date**

   j. Display the **slide number** in the footer area at the bottom right of the slide.

   k. Make sure the contents of the footer area do not touch or overlap the image and that they will be displayed clearly on all the slides.

   l. Format the background to **white**.

   m. Save the presentation using the filename **outlet1**.

## BUILD-UP TASK 2 — Enter data on slides and print slides

Continue working on your saved presentation **outlet1**. Make sure that you are in Normal view.

1. Create slide 1 and enter the title: **BX Retail Centre**
2. Enter the following text in the main placeholder with the style shown:

   | | |
   |---|---|
   | **Now Open!** | first-level bullet |

3. You should not use a title slide layout and you must not have a blank slide as slide 1.
4. Create slide 2 and enter the title: **Retail Outlets**
5. Enter the following text in the main placeholder with the styles shown:

   | | |
   |---|---|
   | **Major department stores** | first-level bullet |
   | **Lauren's** | second-level bullet |
   | **OK Bazaar** | second-level bullet |
   | **Miekles** | second-level bullet |
   | **7 restaurants** | second-level bullet |
   | **Cinema** | first-level bullet |

6. Create slide 3 and enter the title: **Amenities**
7. Enter the following text in the main placeholder with the styles shown:

   | | |
   |---|---|
   | **Free parking** | first-level bullet |
   | **Courtesy buses** | second-level bullet |
   | **Open 7 days** | first-level bullet |
   | **Retail hours extended** | first-level bullet |

8. Use the spell check facility to check the accuracy of the text.
9. Save the slide show keeping the filename **outlet1**.
10. Print out each of the three slides, one per page, in landscape orientation.

Unit 5: Create an e-presentation

## BUILD-UP TASK 3  *Update a presentation*

Continue working on your presentation **outlet1**. You will need to make some changes to your presentation.

1 On slide 2, delete the line **Miekles**.

2 Add the following line to slide 3, after **Retail hours extended**:

   **24 hour security**      second-level bullet

3 On slide 2, promote the line **7 restaurants** to become a first-level bullet.

4 Create slide 4 and enter the title: **Parent and Baby**

5 In the main placeholder create an arrow pointing to the left as shown below.

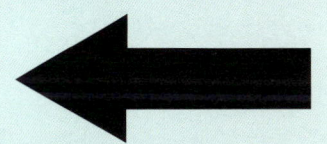

   ○ Fill this arrow with black.

   ○ Make sure the arrow does not touch or overlap the image or any text.

   ○ Make sure it is displayed between the title and the footer area.

6 Save the presentation with the new filename **outlet2**.

7 Print the slides as **handouts** with all slides on one page.

## BUILD-UP TASK 4  *Update a presentation*

The presentation **outlet2** needs updating.

1 In your presentation **outlet2**, change the order of the slides so that slide 4 becomes slide 3.

2 Replace the word **Retail** with the word **Shopping** wherever it appears in the presentation (three times in all). Make sure you match the use of case.

3 Save the amended presentation using the new filename **outlet3**

4 An Outline view printout will be needed.

   ○ Enter **your name** as a header or footer for this print.

   ○ Print the presentation in **Outline** view to display the text on all four slides.

   ○ Make sure you check your printouts for accuracy.

5 Close the presentation and exit PowerPoint.

You should have the following printouts:

   ○ three individual slides

   ○ a handout print showing all four slides

   ○ an Outline view print of all four slides.

## PRACTICE TASK: *Create a master slide*

### Task 1

You will need the image **crest** from the folder **files_presentations**.

### Scenario

You are working as an administrative assistant at a local swimming pool. You have been asked to produce a slide show presentation about a training course for pool lifeguards.

1. Set up a master slide as follows. This master slide layout must be used for all the slides.

   a. Set the slide orientation to **landscape**.

   b. Use the placeholder at the top of the slide for the title.

   c. Use the main placeholder for the slide content.

   d. Set up the text styles as follows:

   | STYLE | EMPHASIS | SIZE | FEATURE | ALIGNMENT |
   | --- | --- | --- | --- | --- |
   | title | bold only | large | dark border | centre |
   | first-level bullet | none | medium | any bullet character | left |
   | second-level bullet | italic only | small | any bullet character | left indented from first-level bullet |

   e. Make sure there is at least one character space between the bullets and the text.

   f. In the footer area enter:

   your name

   your centre number

   an automatic date.

   g. Display the **slide number** in the footer area at the bottom right of the slide.

   h. Format the background to **white**.

2. Save the presentation using the filename **lifegd1**

Unit 5: Create an e-presentation

# PRACTICE TASK  *Enter data on slides and print slides*

## Task 2

Continue working on your saved presentation **lifegd1**. Make sure you are in Normal view and that you enter text in upper and lower case as shown.

1. Create slide 1 and enter the title below. The title may be displayed on two lines:

   **POOL LIFEGUARD TRAINING**

2. Insert the image **crest** below the title placeholder in the centre of the slide. You may resize this image.

3. Create slide 2 and enter the title: **RESPONSIBILITIES**

4. Enter the following text in the main placeholder with the styles shown:

   | | |
   |---|---|
   | **Supervision** | first-level bullet |
   | **Poolside** | second-level bullet |
   | **Changing Rooms** | second-level bullet |
   | **Emergency Procedures** | first-level bullet |
   | **Poolside Accidents** | second-level bullet |
   | **Aquatic Accidents** | second-level bullet |
   | **Basic First Aid** | second-level bullet |

5. Create slide 3 and enter the title: **EQUIPMENT PROVIDED**

6. Enter the following text in the main placeholder with the styles shown:

   | | |
   |---|---|
   | **First Aid Box** | first-level bullet |
   | **Accidents Book** | first-level bullet |
   | **Spinal Board** | first-level bullet |
   | **Throw-ins** | first-level bullet |
   | **Buoys** | second-level bullet |
   | **Ropes** | second-level bullet |

7. Use the spell check facility to check the accuracy of the text.

8. Save the slide show keeping the filename **lifegd1**.

9. Print the presentation as **handouts** with three slides to a page.

## PRACTICE TASK  *Update a presentation*

### Task 3

Continue working on your presentation **lifegd1**. The Pool Manager has asked you to make a few changes to the presentation.

1. On slide 2 entitled **RESPONSIBILITIES**, promote the line **Basic First Aid** to become a first-level bullet.
2. Replace the word **Accidents** with the word **Incidents** wherever it appears in the presentation (three times in all). Make sure you match the use of case.
3. Create a new slide as slide 4 and enter the title: **ENROLMENT**
4. In the main placeholder, create the shape of a callout box similar to that shown below.

   - Fill this shape with a dark colour.
   - Make sure it does not touch or overlap the image or any text.
   - Make sure it is displayed between the title and the footer area.

5. Save the presentation using the new filename **lifegd2**
6. Print slides 2 and 4 as individual slides, one per page.

## PRACTICE TASK  *Update a presentation*

### Task 4

Continue working on your presentation **lifegd2**.

1. On slide 2, titled **RESPONSIBILITIES**, delete the line **Changing Rooms**.
2. Change the order of the slides so that slide 2 becomes slide 3.
3. Save the amended presentation using the new filename **lifegd3**
4. An Outline view printout will be needed.
   - Enter **your name** as a header or footer for this print.
   - Print the presentation in **Outline** view. This must display only the text on all four slides and your name.
   - Make sure you check your printouts for accuracy.
5. Run the presentation from slide 1 (optional).
6. Close the presentation and exit PowerPoint.

You should have the following printouts:
- a handout print showing slides 1, 2 and 3
- two individual slides
- an Outline view print showing slides 1, 2, 3 and 4.

# UNIT 5: Create an e-presentation

## Definition of terms

| | |
|---|---|
| **Alignment** | How data lines up with the left and right sides of the placeholder. Text can be aligned to the left, centre or right. |
| **Amend** | To make changes to data. Also referred to as 'edit'. |
| **Audience notes** | A handout print that displays miniatures of the slides. Also referred to as 'handouts'. |
| **Background** | The area behind text and images on slides. The background may be a solid colour, a pattern or a picture. |
| **Bullet** | A character of any style that is used to display a list of items. Examples of bullet characters are:<br>• <br>✓<br>✗ |
| **Data** | Text, numbers or images that are inserted into a presentation. |
| **Delete** | To remove text or images completely from a presentation. |
| **Demote** | To indent a bullet point so that it is set further in from the left margin to become a lower-level bullet point. |
| **Distort** | To change the original proportions (shape) of an image. |
| **Drawing toolbar** | A toolbar that is usually displayed at the bottom of the screen. It displays icons for common drawing items (e.g. AutoShapes). |
| **Find and replace** | A technique where PowerPoint searches for a particular word in a presentation and replaces that word with another word. |
| **Folder** | A storage area in which files can be saved. Creating folders with suitable names allows computer files to be organised logically. |
| **Format** | The layout and appearance of text (e.g. bold, italic, etc.). |
| **Handle** | Small circles that display in the corners and at the sides of a placeholder or an image. Handles are used to resize objects. |
| **Handouts** | A printout displaying the slides in a presentation as miniatures. A handout print can display two, three, four, six or nine slides on a page. The more slides that are displayed, the smaller the size of the miniature. Also referred to as thumbnails, or audience notes. |
| **Insert slide** | To add a new slide to a presentation. |

| | |
|---|---|
| **Master slide** | A template. A master slide is used to place standard items (e.g. headers and footers and images) and to format text consistently to ensure that a presentation looks professional. |
| **Miniature** | A smaller version of a slide. |
| **Outline view** | A printout that displays only the text on the slides (i.e. text entered into the title and main placeholders). Text entered into headers and footers on the master slide and images, etc., do not print on an Outline view printout. |
| **Outlining toolbar** | A toolbar that is usually displayed on the left of the screen. It contains the icons for Promote and Demote. |
| **Overlap** | A placeholder, image or text touches or is partially placed over another item (e.g. text, image or placeholder). |
| **Placeholder** | A frame (box) that contains text, images, headers and footers, etc. On the screen a placeholder is surrounded by a border so that the placeholder can be seen easily. However, these borders do not print. |
| **Presentation** | A number of slides. |
| **Promote** | To increase the indent of a second-level bullet point so that it becomes a higher-level bullet point. |
| **Slides** | A presentation is made up of a number of slides. Each slide is displayed as a full page. |
| **Slide layout** | A slide display preset by PowerPoint. Using a preset layout for all slides helps to make sure that all text, images and footers, etc., are displayed consistently on all the slides. |
| **Slide master** | The term used by PowerPoint for a master slide. |
| **Slide show** | A preview of the presentation where each slide is displayed on a full screen with no menus, toolbars, etc. An audience would view a slide show with one slide displayed on the screen at a time. |
| **Task pane** | A section usually located on the right-hand side of the screen. It displays a selection of slide layouts. |
| **Thumbnail** | A miniature of a slide. |
| **User area** | The workspace on a computer for a user to save files. Examples of user areas are My Documents, a network drive, the floppy disk drive or C drive. |
| **Views** | Different ways of viewing a presentation on the screen. The most commonly used views are Normal, Slide Sorter and Slide Show. |

# Preparation for the assessment

## General assessment guidelines for all units

### Before the assessment

Before you start a live assessment, complete at least two 'mock exams' in assessment conditions, without any help from your tutor or classmates.

### The assessment

- Level 1 assessments are usually split into four tasks.
- You are allowed a notional duration of 2½ hours for each assessment.
- Before you begin, read through the paper to see what you will need to do.
- You may want to allow yourself about half an hour for each task and then half an hour to check all your final printouts and your saved files.
- Your tutor may allow you to complete an assessment over several consecutive sessions (lessons).
- Once you start an assessment your tutor cannot give you further teaching and is not allowed to help you, so make sure that you are ready for the assessment before starting a live assessment.
- Your tutor will provide you with a photocopy of the original assignment.
- Printing can be done after the assessment, however, you are advised to print your work whenever there is an instruction to print.

### TIP!

When you have printed your work, do not move straight on to the next instruction or task! Check your printout against the instructions in the assignment to make absolutely sure that you have carried out each instruction correctly and that the printout matches what you have on the screen.

### Your name

In many assignments you will be asked to enter your name and centre number, it is good practice to enter your first and last name.

### Filenames

You are advised to enter filenames using the same case as in the assignment. However, you will not be penalised if you use a different case for filenames. Do not enter a full stop after a file or folder name.

### During the assessment

- During the assessment you are allowed to use:
  - the Heinemann textbook you worked through when you were learning about PowerPoint
  - the **Quick reference guides** from the Heinemann book
  - your own notes

- handouts from your tutor that cover general IT skills
- any books that cover general IT skills.

○ You are not allowed to use any books, notes, handouts, etc. that are referenced to the assessment objectives of the syllabus.

○ You cannot ask your tutor or anyone else for help.

○ If there is a technical problem (e.g. there is something wrong with the computer or printer), then you should inform your tutor or the invigilator.

○ Read through the whole task before you start.

○ All the instructions are numbered, and many have sub-steps (a, b, c, etc.). Read through the whole step before you start doing anything.

○ Follow each instruction in the correct sequence. Do not leave out an instruction, even if you intend to do it later.

○ Tick each instruction when you have completed it.

○ Check that you have completed a step fully and correctly before moving on to the next step.

○ Don't rush!

○ Enter all data in the same case (i.e. capital/small letters) as in the assignment.

○ Enter all data as it is presented in the assignment. Ignore any alternative spelling or grammar suggestions made by PowerPoint.

○ Any data that you have to type in is presented in bold to help you see what you have to key in. You should not use bold emphasis unless you are told to do so in the assessment.

○ Make sure the spell checker is switched on before you start and do a spell check again when you finish.

○ If you find an error you can correct it, but if you leave the checking to your tutor, they cannot give your work back to you to correct any errors that they have found.

○ If you notice an error, you can make changes to your work and print again.

○ You can print as many draft copies as you wish, but you must remember to destroy any rough or incorrect copies.

○ Where there is an instruction to enter your name or to add your name to a file or folder name, then you must use your own first and last name, not the words 'your name'.

○ You may display your centre number in any format, e.g. Centre 11111, Centre No. 11111, etc.

> **TIP!**
>
> Saving: read through all the instructions for the task before you start work. If you are required to save the presentation with a different filename, then do so before you start the task. This way you will not save over a file used for the previous task.

**At the end of the assessment**

○ Check your printout against the assessment paper. Use a different colour pen/pencil to tick against each instruction in the assessment.

○ Make sure that you have saved all your files.

- Make sure that have saved using the correct filename.
- Make sure that all your files are saved in the correct user area.
- Make sure that every printout has your first and last name on it.
- Arrange your prints – put the final correct version of each printout in the order that they are listed in the assessment.
- Destroy any printouts that you do not wish to be marked (or hand these to your tutor, making sure that your tutor knows these are not to be marked!).

Hand to your tutor:

- your final printouts in the correct order. You may wish to staple these to keep them secure
- the copy of the assessment paper
- the disk where you have saved your files (if you save them on disk). If not, tell the tutor where your files are saved on the computer.

## Assessment guidelines for Unit 5

1  Your tutor will provide you with the image file that you will need.
2  Before an assessment you should create a new folder just for the assessment.

### e-presentation tasks

There will usually be four tasks.

1  You will usually create a master slide. On the master slide you will be instructed to format the style for the title, first-level text and second-level text; to format the background; to set the slide orientation; and to insert headers and footers, slide numbers and an image. In some assignments, you may insert an image into an individual slide instead of into the master slide. You will be instructed to save the presentation using a specified filename.

2  You will usually enter text on three slides, save and print the presentation.

3  You will then update the presentation. You will usually be instructed to insert a fourth slide and to draw a graphic shape (AutoShape) on this slide, then fill the shape with a colour. You will need to find and replace text, delete text, insert text, promote and/or demote text. While updating the presentation, you will be instructed to save the updated presentation using a different filename. At the end of the assignment, you will normally have three presentations.

4  During the assignment, you will normally need to print three times. Each time you will be instructed to print in a different style:

- print all the slides or selected slides as individual slides
- print as handouts with three or four slides on one page
- print an Outline view print. There will usually be an instruction before this print to insert your name (and centre number) into the Outline view print.

### Create a master slide

- You will create a new blank presentation. Make sure you start a new presentation. Do not be tempted to use an existing presentation in which you have already created a master slide.

- To create a master slide, you must go to Slide Master view.
- Make sure you carry out each instruction carefully. All the slides in a presentation are based on the master slide, so you must make sure that the master slide is created correctly. Any errors on the master slide will appear on every slide in the presentation.
- Make sure you carry out each of the formatting instructions for the title, first-level text and second-level text.
- Also make sure that you check the 'feature' column to see what features to use.
- While creating the master slide, you are advised to switch frequently to Normal view to check the layout, positioning and format of items.
- When entering your name on the master slide, enter your own first and last name, not the words 'your name'.
- Make sure you know what your centre number is before you begin the assessment. Do not confuse your centre number with any other candidate registration numbers. Centre numbers usually have five digits.
- You are advised to enter your name and centre number via the Header and Footer dialogue box. However, these can also be entered directly into the master slide in the footer placeholder.
- When inserting an automatic date or the date and time, make sure you click the button for **Update automatically**.
- Make sure you save the presentation using the correct filename.
- Make sure that you save all your assessment presentations into the user area for the assessment instead of into your usual user area. You are advised to enter filenames using the same case as in the assignment. However, you will not be penalised for the different use of case for filenames.

Before you insert any new slides, switch to Normal view. With the slide displayed in Normal view, check that you have carried out each instruction about setting up the master slide. Tick off each instruction on the assessment paper. Make sure that you have carried out each instruction for setting up the text styles – these are usually presented in a table and so it is easy to miss out an instruction.

- Avoid using unusual bullet character styles. Some styles do not display the space after the bullet character clearly.

**Enter text on slides**

- You must check that you are in Normal view before you insert a new slide and before you enter any text on any slides.
- Remember that PowerPoint always displays a Title Slide as the first slide. You must not use a Title Slide layout for the first slide or for any slides. All slides must have a consistent layout (i.e. the position of all placeholders must be the same on all the slides).
- When you insert a new slide, make sure that the Title and Text layout is selected.
- In the Slides pane, delete the Title Slide layout.

Before you enter any text on slide 1, make sure that:

- you have only one slide in your presentation
- the blank title slide has been deleted
- you are using a Title and Text slide layout.

- Make sure you enter text in exactly the same case as shown.
- Do not enter the text in bold: the text is presented in bold to help you to see what to type. You will have already set up the styles on the master slide. You should not apply any formatting on individual slides.
- Do not press the spacebar, the Enter key or the Tab key at the end of the title. Click with your mouse in the main placeholder.
- After you have entered the text in the main placeholder, check to make sure that you have displayed the bullet text at first or second level as instructed.
- Every time you insert a new slide, check that the Title and Text layout is selected.
- Always use spell check before you save.
- You will normally be instructed to print after you have entered text on three or four slides. Make sure you print *only* the slides specified and that you print the correct layout (individual slides, handouts or Outline view). If you are printing handouts, make sure that you set the option for the number of slides to be displayed on one page.
- Check the first set of printouts before proceeding. If you need to make a change on the master slide, you must do so before continuing with the assignment.
- Remember, if you do make any amendments to the master slide, you must print again.
- Check that headers and footers have printed correctly on an Outline view print.

**Update the presentation**

- Save the updated presentation with the new filename before you start working through the instructions. This is just in case you click the Save button by mistake!
- When you replace a word, remember to click the button for **Match case** and the button for **Find whole words only**. Remember to use **Replace All** (not Replace).

Check all printouts for accuracy.

Good luck!

# Index

alignment   11, 12, 13, 14

backgrounds, applying consistently   23
borders/boxes   14–16

colours
   background   23
   borders/boxes   15–16
   filling graphic shapes   49

demoting text   34–6, 50
Drawing toolbar   14–15, 47–8

editing a presentation   44–52
emphasising text   11, 12, 13, 14
entering text   7–8, 32–3, 46

Find and Replace   50–1
first-level text, setting style of   12–13

graphic shapes
   colouring   49
   drawing   47–8

handouts, printing   38
headers and footers   23–5, 42

images
   inserting   17–19
   positioning   19–22
   resizing   20
inserting new slides   29–30, 33–4, 47

keyboard, using   7–8

language settings   37
lines, drawing   14–15

master slide
   creating   8–9
   inserting images   17–19
   positioning images   19–22
   resizing images   20
   text styles, setting   11–14
   View toolbar   9–10
menus, using   5
mouse techniques   3

Normal view   22, 25

orientation, of slides   10
Outline view   38
Outlining toolbar   34–5

placeholders
   deleting   45–6
   moving   21
Powerpoint
   exiting   26
   menus   5
   print options   38
   starting   3–4
   task pane, closing   6

views   25
window   4–5, 6
*see also* toolbars
presentations   2–3
   closing   26
   opening   28–9
   printing   38–43
   running   52–3
   saving   16–17, 44–5
printing
   handouts   38, 39, 41–2
   individual slides   38, 40
   Outline view   38, 39, 42–3
   selected slides   39
promoting text   34–5, 50

running a presentation   52–3

saving a presentation   16–17
second-level text, setting style of   13–14
shapes, drawing   47–8
size of text, setting   12, 13, 14
Slide Show view   25
Slide Sorter view   25
slides
   entering data   29–38
   layout, consistency of   31
   navigation   47
   order, changing   51
   orientation   10
   updating   44–52
   viewing   25
   *see also* master slide
spell checking   36–8
sub-bullet text   34

task pane, closing   6
text
   deleting   44
   demoting   34–6, 50
   emphasising   11, 12, 13, 14
   entering   7–8, 32–3, 46
   Find and Replace   50–1
   positioning   21–2
   promoting   34–5, 50
text styles, master slide
   first-level text   12–13
   second-level text   13–14
   title   11–12
title text, setting style of   11–12
title slide, deleting   31
toolbars
   Drawing   14–15, 47–8
   Outlining   34–5
   Slide Master View   9–10
   Standard and Formatting   6–7

updating a presentation   44–52

viewing slides, different ways of   25